A Mariner's Guide to the Rules of the Road

A Mariner's Guide to the Rules of the Road

Second Edition

William H. Tate

Naval Institute Press
Annapolis, Maryland

Library of Congress Cataloging in Publication Data

Tate, William Henry, 1945-
    A mariner's guide to the rules of the road.

    1. Rule of the road at sea.   2. Inland naviga-
tion—United States—Laws and regulations.
3. Navigation—Safety measures.   I. Title.
VK371.T37   1982   623.88′84   81-85441
ISBN 0-87021-355-5   AACR2

Printed in the United States of America

To my turkeys
Tania and Michelle

Contents

Preface to the
Second Edition

The second edition of *A Mariner's Guide to the Rules of the Road* uses an entirely new format in order to take advantage of the *similarities* between the new Inland Rules and the 1972 International Rules or COLREGS. The significant *differences* which remain are in the signals used for power-driven vessels meeting, crossing, and overtaking. The chapters on these situations first define the situation, the situations being defined in the same way in both sets of rules. The Inland signals and actions are then described, followed by the signals and actions required by the COLREGS.

On 19 November 1981 the Intergovernmental Maritime Safety Committee adopted a resolution to amend the 1972 COLREGS, incorporating changes which would resolve some of the differences between the COLREGS and the new Inland Rules. Since the amendments, after approval by two-thirds of the contracting governments, will go into force on 1 June 1983, they have been made part of the text to keep the book entirely up to date.

William H. Tate
Lieutenant Commander, U.S. Naval Reserve
800 N. River Dr.
Stuart, FL 33494

Any opinions or assertions contained in this text are those of the author and do not necessarily reflect the views of the Navy or the naval service as a whole.

Acknowledgements to the First Edition

The contents of this text were originally discussed at a Navigation Symposium held in Newport, Rhode Island, in April of 1973. The author is especially grateful to Commander F. E. Bassett, USN, Chairman of the Navigation Department at the U.S. Naval Academy, under whose guidance this text was prepared, and to the following officers who continually made their contributions and suggestions during the preparation of the text: Lieutenant Commander J. L. Roberts, USN, Lieutenant Commander A. J. Tuttle, USN, and Lieutenant Commander R. A. Smith, RN. Special thanks are also due to other members of the marine community who have made suggestions and contributions: Captain J. C. Martin, USN (Ret.), Defense Mapping Agency; Captain C. J. McGuire, USCG, U.S. Coast Guard Headquarters; Captain R. H. Terry and Commander E. J. Geissler, USCG (Ret.), Maine Maritime Academy; Captain E. D. Cassidy, USCG, U.S. Coast Guard Academy; Professor Lester A. Dutcher, State University of New York Maritime College; and Commander O. E. Thompson, USMS, U.S. Merchant Marine Academy.

A Mariner's Guide
to the
Rules of the Road

1 Introduction to the Rules of the Road

The navigation of a vessel on the high seas (or in the inland waters of any nation having no special rules) is subject to the International Regulations for Preventing Collisions at Sea (commonly called the International Rules of the Road or COLREGS). The 1972 Rules Conference which produced the most recent revision of the COLREGS marked the conclusion of four years of effort by national committees and international working groups. One of the foremost desires of those groups was that the rules be simplified and aimed at the mariner, not at those who practice admiralty law. The intent of the rules is to provide the mariner with a practical code for safely maneuvering a ship with relation to others. Fifty-two governments participated in the conference, under the auspices of the Intergovernmental Maritime Consultative Organization (IMCO). Previous revisions were made by similar conferences in 1948 and 1960. The COLREGS are given force by separate statutes in each of the participating maritime nations.

Rule 1 of the COLREGS begins as follows:

These rules shall apply to all vessels upon the high seas and in all waters connected therewith navigable by seagoing vessels.

Nothing in these rules shall interfere with the operation of special rules made by an appropriate authority for roadsteads, harbours, rivers, lakes or inland waterways connected with the high seas and navigable by seagoing vessels. Such special rules shall conform as closely as possible to these rules.

The special rules which apply to the inland waters of the United States are called the "Inland Rules." The "Inland Navigational Rules Act of 1980" provides a set of rules that unifies the old Inland Rules, Great Lakes Rules, and Western Rivers Rules. The effective date of the new Inland Rules is December 24, 1981.

The new Inland Rules use the same format and numbering as the COLREGS. They further reduce confusion with the COLREGS by eliminating major differences in lights and shapes, right of

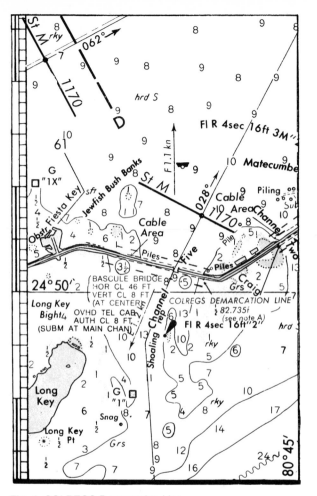

Fig. 1 COLREGS Demarcation Line.

way provisions, fog signals, and other signals such as the danger signal and bend signal. The Coast Guard should be commended for these accomplishments because they significantly aid the mariner. Major differences, however, remain in the signals for power-driven vessels meeting, crossing, and overtaking. The signals in the Inland Rules retain the meaning of intent-agreement from the old rules.

The purpose of the rules of the road is to prevent collisions. Captain Raymond F. Farwell, author of *Rules of the Nautical Road*, 1940, noted that "nearly all marine collisions follow violations of the rules of the road. The inference is that the rules, if implicitly obeyed, are practically collision-proof." Officers at sea must have such a thorough understanding of the rules that they can recognize each situation and know the actions required of their vessel without hesitation.

GENERAL PRINCIPLES

The following general principles emphasize the importance of the rules and assist in placing the rules in the proper perspective:

Rules apply according to location of vessel;
Rules of the road are mandatory;
Obedience must be timely;
Rules apply alike to all vessels.

RULES APPLY ACCORDING TO LOCATION OF VESSEL

The boundary lines which separate the waters subject to the Inland Rules from the waters subject to the COLREGS are called COLREGS demarcation lines. They are normally shown on navigational charts. When planning a voyage to a foreign country, a mariner should consult the *Sailing Directions* in order to become familiar with the special rules (if any) for the waters to be traversed. Because of the differences between the COLREGS and any set of special rules, it is extremely important that the mariner be familiar with the rules that apply to the geographic location of the vessel, and be aware of a boundary whenever approaching it.

RULES OF THE ROAD ARE MANDATORY

Both the COLREGS and the Inland Rules are statutory—they are laws which can be found in Title 33 of the United States Code. Because enforcement is generally not feasible, the COLREGS contain no penalty for violations. The Inland Rules, however, provide for a penalty for vessels navigated in violation of the rules and regulations:

SEC. 4.

(a) Whoever operates a vessel in violation of this Act, or of any regulation issued thereunder, or in violation of a certificate of alternative compliance issued under Rule 1 is liable to a civil penalty of not more than $5,000 for each violation.

(b) Every vessel subject to this act, other than a public vessel being used for noncommercial purposes, that is operated in violation of this Act, or of any regulation issued thereunder, or in violation of a certificate of alternative compliance issued under Rule 1 is liable to a civil penalty of not more than $5,000 for each violation, for which penalty the vessel may be seized and proceeded against in the district court of the United States of any district within which the vessel may be found.

(c) The Secretary may assess any civil penalty authorized by this section. No such penalty may be assessed until the person charged, or the owner of the vessel charged, as appropriate, shall have been given notice of the violation involved and an opportunity for a hearing. For good cause shown, the Secretary may remit, mitigate, or compromise any penalty assessed. Upon the failure of the person charged, or the owner of the vessel charged, to pay an assessed penalty, as it may have been mitigated or compromised, the Secretary may request the Attorney General to commence an action in the appropriate district court of the United States for collection of the penalty as assessed, without regard to the amount involved, together with such other relief as may be appropriate.

(d) The Secretary of the Treasury shall withhold or revoke, at the request of the Secretary, the clearance, required by section 4197 of the Revised Statutes of the United States (46 U.S.C. 91) of any vessel, the owner or operator of which is subject to any of the penalties in this section. Clearance may be granted in such cases upon the filing of a bond or other surety satisfactory to the Secretary.

Both sets of rules are applied by courts of law to determine how damages will be divided by vessels involved in collisions.

The Inland Rules permit the Secretary of the department in which the Coast Guard is operating to issue "regulations necessary to implement and interpret this Act," and they direct the Secretary to establish four technical annexes to the rules: Annex I, Positioning and Technical Details of

Lights and Shapes; Annex II, Additional Signals for Fishing Vessels Fishing in Close Proximity; Annex III, Technical Details of Sound Appliances; and Annex IV, Distress Signals. These annexes shall be as consistent as possible with the respective annexes to the COLREGS. The Inland Rules also permit the Secretary to "establish other technical annexes, including local pilot rules." In fact, Annex V to the Inland Rules *is* the Pilot Rules. The Pilot Rules, as well as the other annexes, are not statutory, but are regulations found in the Code of Federal Regulations. Notice that the section of the Inland Rules on violations, quoted above, states that whoever operates a vessel in violation of this act "or of any regulation issued thereunder" is subject to a fine.

The legal status of the Pilot Rules can best be summarized in the words of a district court:

> Pilot Rules promulgated by Coast Guard in accordance with statutory authority are valid unless inconsistent with statutory rules, and, if valid, have force of law.[1]

Thus the mariner is governed by the statutory COLREGS and Inland rules, and the Pilot Rules which have the force of law. There are only two grounds on which departure from the rules will be excused by the courts. The first is given by Rule 2(b) (COLREGS and Inland Rules):

> In construing and complying with these rules due regard shall be had to all dangers of navigation and collision and to any special circumstances, including the limitations of the vessels involved, which may make a departure from these rules necessary to avoid immediate danger.

1. *Compania Carreto De Navigation, S.A.* v. *Tug Sagamore*, D.C.N.Y. 1963, 223 F. Supp. 598.

Secondly, a departure from the rules which was not required by special circumstances will be excused only if the offending vessel can show that such departure could not have contributed to the collision. As expressed by a court of appeals:

> When fault consists in breach of statutory rule intended to prevent collisions, burden rests upon ship of not showing merely that her fault might not have been one of causes, or that it probably was not, but that it could not have been.[2]

OBEDIENCE MUST BE TIMELY

The rules make this requirement very definite:

Rule 8—Action to Avoid Collision
(a) Any action taken to avoid collision shall, if the circumstances of the case admit, be positive, made in ample time and with due regard to the observance of good seamanship.
(b) Any alteration of course or speed to avoid collision shall, if the circumstances of the case admit, be large enough to be readily apparent to another vessel observing visually or by radar; a succession of small alterations of course or speed should be avoided.
(c) If there is sufficient sea room, alteration of course alone may be the most effective action to avoid a close-quarters situation provided that it is made in good time, is substantial and does not result in another close-quarters situation.
(d) Action taken to avoid collision with another vessel shall be such as to result in passing at a safe distance. The effectiveness of the action shall be carefully checked until the other vessel is finally past and clear.

2. *Diesel Tanker F.A. Verdon, Inc.* v. *Stakeboat No. 2*, C.A.N.Y. 1965, 340 F. 2d 465.

(e) If necessary to avoid collision or allow more time to assess the situation, a vessel shall slacken her speed or take all way off by stopping or reversing her means of propulsion.

An old ruling shows that the courts have long required that obedience be timely:

> Precautions required by law to be taken when there is a risk of collision must be taken in time to be effective against such risk, or they will constitute no defense if collision occurs.[3]

RULES APPLY ALIKE TO ALL VESSELS

All vessels, public and private, regardless of size, speed, or nationality, must obey the rules.

PRINCIPLES OF MARINE COLLISION LAW

The purpose of this section is to familiarize the reader with certain principles of marine collision law as exercised in the courts of the United States.

RULES MODIFIED BY COURT INTERPRETATION

Rule 2(a) states that special circumstances may require precautions in addition to the literal requirements of the rules. Consequently, over the years numerous court decisions have addressed these circumstances and construed various rules with the requirements of Rule 2(a) (*see* Chapter 10). The courts have also provided legal meanings for certain phrases used in the rules, such as "proper lookout" and "risk of collision." It is because of the necessity to understand the rules in light of court interpretation that texts such as this one exist.

3. The *Westhall*, D.C. Va. 1899, 153 F. 1010.

JURISDICTION IN COLLISION CASES

Federal courts, sitting as courts of admiralty, have jurisdiction over cases of collision between vessels on public navigable waters (defined as waters used, or capable of being used, in interstate commerce). Collision cases begin in a federal district court, and can be appealed to a circuit court of appeals, and in some cases, to the United States Supreme Court.

State courts have jurisdiction when collisions occur on a lake wholly within a state; they have concurrent jurisdiction when collisions occur in any portion of public navigable waters within a state. The majority of the latter cases are tried in federal courts.

LEGAL PERSONALITY OF A VESSEL

In courts of the United States a vessel is assumed to be the wrongdoer when collision follows a violation of the rules of the road. When a vessel is libeled, she is sued "in rem." The vessel is taken into custody until the claims against her are satisfied, unless the owners obtain her release by paying an amount equal to her appraised valuation, or posting a bond double the amount of existing liens. A vessel may be sold to satisfy the judgment against her. The sale gives the vessel a new lease on life, as the owners are free of any old claims against her.

Naval vessels and other public vessels are not subject to lien and cannot be taken into custody. The United States is sued as an owner "in personam," rather than the vessel being sued "in rem."

LIMITED LIABILITY OF A VESSEL

The principle of limited liability serves to protect the owner against the possibility of losing all of his resources because of a negligent master. In the United States, the limit of liability is the value of the vessel after the incident giving rise to the claim, plus pending freight. The limit may be computed differently in other countries. It is possible, then, that a vessel totally at fault, but also totally lost and with no pending freight, could leave the injured vessel unable to recover anything for damage either to herself or her cargo. A vessel's liability for damage to her own cargo is governed by the Harter Act and the later Carriage of Goods by Sea Act. The so-called Morro Castle amendment limits the liability for death or personal injury to a maximum of $60 per gross register ton where the remaining value of the ship is less than that amount.

If the circumstances of a collision or other casualty are found to be due to the fault or privity of the owners, limitation of liability can be denied. In such a case, levies can be placed against the owner's entire fleet, if necessary, to satisfy a judgment. Liability for environmental damage is governed by the Federal Water Pollution Control Act in the United States and the 1969–71 oil pollution convention with regard to many maritime nations.

COMPARATIVE NEGLIGENCE

For many years the courts of the United States required two vessels involved in a collision to share the total damages equally if both were guilty of a rule violation that contributed to the collision. In 1975 the Supreme Court adopted what might be called a rule of comparative negligence:

We hold that when two or more parties have contributed by their fault to cause property damage in a maritime collision or stranding, liability for such damage is to be allocated among the parties proportionately to the comparative degree of their fault, and that liability for such damages is to be allocated equally only when the parties are equally at fault or when it is not possible fairly to measure the comparative degree of their fault.[4]

If one vessel is solely at fault, she is liable for the total damage to the other, subject only to the provisions of the Limited Liability Acts.

INEVITABLE COLLISION

If neither vessel is found at fault in a collision, each must bear its own loss. Such cases are rare; the following rulings illustrate the thinking of the courts:

Finding that collision between vessels was result of inevitable accident is not to be lightly arrived at, and the burden of proof is heavily upon party asserting that defense to affirmatively establish that accident could not have been prevented by use of that degree of reasonable care and attention which the situation demanded, and that there was no intervening act of negligence on its part.[5]

Where a collision between steamships occurs, exclusive of natural causes and without the fault of either party, the loss must rest where it falls, but such a case requires that both parties must have endeavored by every means in their power, with due care and caution and a proper display of nautical skill, to prevent the collision.[6]

4. *U.S.* v. *Reliable Transfer Company, Inc.*, 1975, 44 L. Ed. 251.
5. *Swenson* v. *The Argonaut*, C.A.N.J. 1953, 204 F. 2d 636.
6. The *Djerissa*, D.C. Va. 1919, 2558 F. 949, affirmed 267 F. 115.

To exonerate a steamer from liability . . . on the ground of inevitable accident arising from a latent defect in her machinery, it must be shown that such defect could not have been discovered by a person of competent skill in the exercise of ordinary care, and further, that such defect necessarily caused the accident.[7]

DEFINITIONS

The following definitions will aid in the discussion of the rules.

Vessel   A water craft of any description, including nondisplacement craft and seaplanes, used or capable of being used as a means of transportation on water.

Power-driven vessel   Any vessel propelled by machinery.

Sailing vessel   Any vessel under sail provided that propelling machinery, if fitted, is not being used.

Vessel engaged in fishing   Any vessel fishing with nets, lines, trawls, or other fishing apparatus which restrict maneuverability. A vessel fishing with trolling lines or other fishing apparatus which do *not* restrict maneuverability does not qualify.

Seaplane   Any aircraft designed to maneuver on the water.

Vessel not under command   A vessel that through some exceptional circumstance is unable to maneuver as required by these rules and is therefore unable to keep out of the way of another vessel.

Vessel restricted in her ability to maneuver   A vessel which from the nature of her work is restricted in her ability to maneuver as required by these Rules and is therefore unable to keep out of the way of another vessel; vessels restricted in their ability to maneuver include, but are not limited to:

(i)   a vessel engaged in laying, servicing, or picking up a navigation mark, submarine cable, or pipeline;

(ii)   a vessel engaged in dredging, surveying, or underwater operations;

(iii)   a vessel engaged in replenishment or transferring persons, provisions, or cargo while underway;

(iv)   a vessel engaged in the launching or recovery of aircraft;

(v)   a vessel engaged in minesweeping operations; and

(vi)   a vessel engaged in a towing operation such as severely restricts the towing vessel and her tow in their ability to deviate from their course.

Underway   Not at anchor, made fast to the shore, or aground.

Length and breadth   A vessel's length overall and greatest breadth.

Restricted visibility   Any condition in which visibility is restricted by fog, mist, falling snow, heavy rainstorms, sandstorms or any other similar causes.

Whistle   Any sound signalling appliance capable of producing the prescribed blasts and which complies with the specifications in Annex III to these regulations.

Short blast   A blast of about one second's duration.

Prolonged blast   A blast of from four to six seconds' duration.

7. The *Homer*, D.C. Wash. 1900, 99 F. 795.

A definition which applies only to the COL-REGS is a *vessel constrained by her draft*. The term means "a power-driven vessel which because of her draft in relation to the available depth of water is severely restricted in her ability to deviate from the course she is following" (Rule 3).

The following definitions apply only to the Inland Rules:

Western Rivers ". . . the Mississippi River, its tributaries, South Pass, and Southwest Pass, to the navigational demarcation lines dividing the high seas from harbors, rivers, and other inland waters of the United States, and the Port Allen-Morgan City Alternate Route, and that part of the Atchafalaya River above its junction with the Port Allen-Morgan City Alternate Route including the Old River and the Red River" (Rule 3(l)).

Great Lakes ". . . the Great Lakes and their connecting and tributary waters including the Calumet River as far as the Thomas J. O'Brien Lock and Controlling Works (between mile 326 and 327), the Chicago River as far as the east side of the Ashland Avenue Bridge (between mile 321 and 322), and the Saint Lawrence River as far east as the lower exit of Saint Lambert Lock" (Rule 3(m)).

Secretary ". . . the Secretary of the department in which the Coast Guard is operating" (Rule 3(n)).

Inland Waters ". . . the navigable waters of the United States shoreward of the navigational demarcation lines dividing the high seas from harbors, rivers, and other inland waters of the United States and the waters of the Great Lakes on the United States side of the International Boundary" (Rule 3(o)).

Inland Rules or *Rules* ". . . the Inland Navigational Rules and the annexes thereto, which govern the conduct of vessels and specify the lights, shapes, and sound signals that apply on inland waters" (Rule 3(p)).

International Regulations ". . . the International Regulations for Preventing Collisions at Sea, 1972, including annexes currently in force for the United States" (Rule 3(q)).

2 Lights and Shapes

The basic purpose of lights is to warn vessels of the presence or approach of other vessels, and to aid in determining the course and aspect of vessels underway. The rules contain a comprehensive hierarchy for "responsibilities between vessels" (right of way). By observing the lights or shapes displayed by an approaching vessel, the mariner can determine which vessel has the responsibility to keep out of the way of the other.

The rules for lights and shapes are found in Part C, Rules 20–31.

Rule 20 — Application

(a) Rules in this part shall be complied with in all weathers.

(b) The Rules concerning lights shall be complied with from sunset to sunrise, and during such times no other lights shall be exhibited, except such lights as cannot be mistaken for the lights specified in these Rules or do not impair their visibility or distinctive character, or interfere with the keeping of a proper lookout.

(c) The lights prescribed by these Rules shall, if carried, also be exhibited from sunrise to sunset in restricted visibility and may be exhibited in all other circumstances when it is deemed necessary.

(d) The Rules concerning shapes shall be complied with by day.

(e) The lights and shapes specified in these Rules shall comply with the provisions of Annex I of these Rules.

Note that lights are *required* to be shown in restricted visibility as well as at night. Lights may also be shown at any other time when deemed necessary.

Certain vessels are required to show additional lights "when making way through the water." *Making way* refers to motion caused by the engines or propelling machinery, not to motion caused by drifting with the current. A vessel which is not at anchor, or made fast to the shore, or aground, while dead in the water, is considered a vessel "underway but stopped and making no way through the water."

TERMS

The following terms will be used in this text to describe the lights and shapes prescribed by the rules. Note that *all the shapes are black*.

Masthead light   A 225° (20-point) light at the forward masthead, showing an arc from dead ahead to 22.5° (2 points) abaft the beam on both sides.

Range light   "Range light" is the term in common use; when used in the rules it is called "a second masthead light abaft of and higher than the forward one." It is a 225° (20-point) white light abaft of and higher than the masthead light. It is in line with the masthead light (forms a range) if the vessel is seen from dead ahead. In every case where the range light is required for a vessel 50 meters and upward in length, it is optional for a vessel less than 50 meters in length. For the sake of brevity, the above details will be omitted from the diagrams on the following pages, and an asterisk (*) shown as a reminder.

Sidelights   A red light on the port side, and a green light on the starboard side. Both are 112.5° (10-point) lights showing from dead ahead to 22.5° (2 points) abaft the beam on their respective sides. Any vessel less than 20 meters in length may combine the sidelights in one lantern.

Sternlight   A 135° (12-point) white light showing 67.5° (6 points) from right aft on each side.

Towing masthead lights   Two or three lights of the same character as the 225° (20-point) masthead light.

Towing range lights   The rules require two or three lights of the same character as the 225° (20-point) range light. They are more commonly used than the towing masthead lights because many of the tugs are designed to put the pilot house as high as possible (limited by bridge clearances) and less glare occurs if the white lights are aft.

Yellow towing light   A 135° (12-point) yellow light, showing over the same arc as a sternlight.

All-round light   A light showing an unbroken light over an arc of the horizon of 360 degrees.

Flashing light   A light flashing at regular intervals at a frequency of 120 flashes or more per minute.

Special flashing light   Inland Rules only—a yellow light flashing at regular intervals at a frequency of 50 to 70 flashes per minute. It is used on the forward end of a tow pushed ahead. Its arc is between 180° to 225° showing an arc from dead ahead to abeam and no more than 22.5° (2 points) abaft the beam on both sides.

Diamond shape   A shape consisting of two cones having a common base.

The lights and shapes prescribed by the rules are illustrated in the following diagrams. The lights and shapes are the same in the COLREGS and Inland Rules *unless otherwise indicated*. While it is occasionally mentioned for clarity that specific lights are the same in both sets of rules, the intention is only to call attention to exceptions. The most significant differences are:

1. The Inland Rules do not have a "vessel constrained by draft."
2. The lights required for vessels engaged in towing vary (for summary *see* pp. 25-26).

Reduced lighting requirements for small vessels are not included in the diagrams (*see* pages 28 and 29).

POWER-DRIVEN VESSELS

Figure 2

Required lights

Masthead light (225°)
Range light   (225°)
Sidelights   (112.5°)
Sternlight   (135°)

An air-cushion vessel operating in the non-displacement mode is required to show a flashing yellow light (all-round) in addition to the above lights.

Note

When a pushing vessel and a vessel being pushed are rigidly connected in a composite unit, they shall be regarded as a power-driven vessel and show the above lights.

Figure 3

Required lights

Masthead light (225°)
Sidelights   (112.5°)
Sternlight   (135°)

An air-cushion vessel operating in the non-displacement mode is required to show a flashing yellow light (all-round) in addition to the above lights.

Other lights

Range light (225°) is optional (not shown in Figure 3).

Note

Same as above

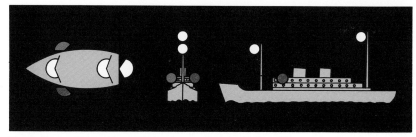

Fig. 2 Power-Driven Vessel (50 meters and upward in length). Rule 23.

Fig. 3 Power-Driven Vessel (Less than 50 meters in length). Rule 23.

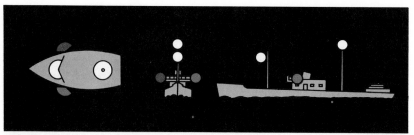

Fig. 4 Power-Driven Vessel—Great Lakes only. Inland Rule 23.

Fig. 5 Sailing Vessel underway. Rule 25.

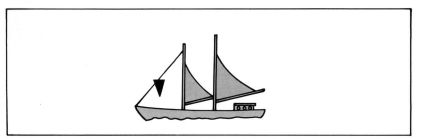

Fig. 6 Vessel proceeding under sail when also being propelled by machinery. Rule 25.

Figure 4 (Great Lakes only)

Required lights
Masthead light (225°)
Sidelights   (112.5°)
All-round white light (in lieu of range light and sternlight)

SAILING VESSELS

Figures 5 and 6

Required lights
Sidelights (112.5°)
Sternlight (135°)

Other lights
Red over green (all-round) at or near the top of the mast, optional.

Note
Small sailing vessels (now defined in both sets of rules as vessels less than 20 meters in length) may combine sidelights and sternlight in one lantern placed at or near the top of the mast. The optional red over green lights may not be shown with such a lantern.

Dayshape
Conical shape, apex down, where best seen. Inland Rules only: optional for vessels less than 12 meters in length.

TOWING ASTERN

Figure 7

Required lights

2 towing masthead lights (225°)

*Range light (225°)—not shown in Figure 7 (*see* page 10)

Sidelights   (112.5°)
Sternlight   (135°)
Yellow towing light   (135°)

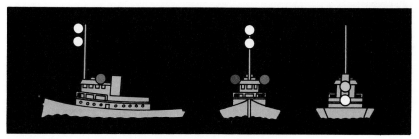

Fig. 7 Towing astern—towing masthead lights. Length of tow does not exceed 200 meters. Rule 24.

Figure 8

Required lights

3 towing masthead lights (225°)

*Range light (225°)—not shown in Figure 8 (*see* page 10)

Sidelights   (112.5°)
Sternlight   (135°)
Yellow towing light   (135°)

Fig. 8 Towing astern—towing masthead lights. Length of tow greater than 200 meters. Rule 24.

Figure 9

Required lights

2 towing range lights   (225°)
Inland only: Masthead light   (225°)
COLREGS only: No masthead light
Sidelights   (112.5°)
Sternlight   (135°)
Yellow towing light   (135°)

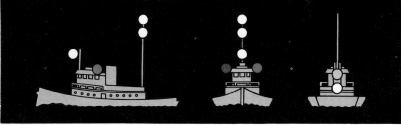

Fig. 9 Towing astern—towing range lights. Length of tow does not exceed 200 meters. The COLREGS do *not* require a masthead light. Rule 24.

Fig. 10 Towing astern—towing range lights. Length of tow is greater than 200 meters. The COLREGS do *not* require a masthead light. Rule 24.

Fig. 11 Pushing ahead or towing alongside—towing masthead lights. Rule 24.

Figure 10

Required lights

3 towing range lights	(225°)
Inland only: Masthead light	(225°)
COLREGS only: No masthead light	
Sidelights	(112.5°)
Sternlight	(135°)
Yellow towing light	(135°)

Dayshape
Diamond where best seen

PUSHING AHEAD OR TOWING ALONGSIDE

Figure 11

Required lights

2 towing masthead lights	(225°)
*Range light (225°)—not shown in Figure 11 (*see* page 10)	
Sidelights	(112.5°)
COLREGS only: Sternlight	(135°)
Inland only: 2 yellow towing lights	(135°)

Note
When a pushing vessel and a vessel being pushed ahead are rigidly connected in a composite unit they shall be regarded as a power-driven vessel and exhibit the lights prescribed in Rule 23.

Pushing Ahead or
Towing Alongside (cont.)

Figure 12 (COLREGS only)

Required lights

2 towing range lights (225°)
Sidelights   (112.5°)
Sternlight   (135°)

Note

Same as above

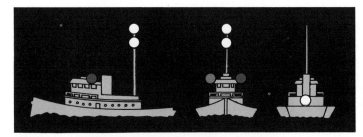

Fig. 12 Pushing ahead or towing alongside—towing range lights. COLREGS only. COLREGS Rule 24.

Figure 13 (Inland only)

Required lights

2 towing range lights (225°)
Masthead light   (225°)
Sidelights   (112.5°)
2 yellow towing lights (135°)

Note

Same as above

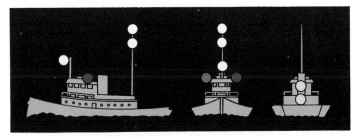

Fig. 13 Pushing ahead or towing alongside—towing range lights. Inland only. Inland Rule 24.

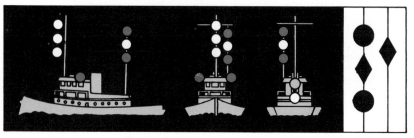

Fig. 14 Towing astern and severely restricted in ability to deviate from course—towing masthead lights. Length of tow greater than 200 meters. Rule 27.

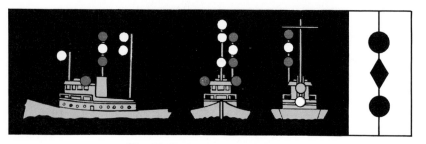

Fig. 15 Towing astern and severely restricted in ability to deviate from course—towing range lights. The COLREGS do *not* require a masthead light. Length of tow does not exceed 200 meters. Rule 27.

TOWING ASTERN AND SEVERELY RESTRICTED IN ABILITY TO DEVIATE FROM COURSE

Figure 14

Required lights

3 towing masthead lights
Red–white–red (all-round) in a vertical line where best seen
*Range light (225°)—not shown in Figure 14 (*see* page 10)
Sidelights   (112.5°)
Sternlight   (135°)
Yellow towing light (135°)

Dayshapes

Ball–diamond–ball in vertical line where best seen
Diamond where best seen

Figure 15

Required lights

2 towing range lights (225°)
Red–white–red (all-round) in a vertical line where best seen
Inland only: Masthead light (225°)
COLREGS only: No masthead light
Sidelights   (112.5°)
Sternlight   (135°)
Yellow towing light   (135°)

Dayshapes

Ball–diamond–ball in a vertical line where best seen

PUSHING AHEAD OR TOWING ALONGSIDE AND SEVERELY RESTRICTED IN ABILITY TO DEVIATE FROM COURSE

Figure 16

Required lights

2 masthead towing lights (225°)

Red–white–red (all-round) in a vertical line where best seen

*Range light (225°)—not shown in Figure 16 (*see* page 10)

Sidelights   (112.5°)

COLREGS only: sternlight (135°)

Inland only: 2 yellow towing lights (135°)

Figure 17

Required lights

2 towing range lights (225°)

Red–white–red (all-round) in a vertical line where best seen

Inland only: Masthead light   (225°)

COLREGS only: No masthead light

Sidelights   (112.5°)

COLREGS only: Sternlight   (135°)

Inland only: 2 yellow towing lights (135°)

Fig. 16 Pushing ahead or towing alongside and severely restricted in ability to deviate from course—COLREGS and Inland. Rule 27.

Fig. 17 Pushing ahead or towing alongside and severely restricted in ability to deviate from course—COLREGS and Inland. Rule 27.

Fig. 18 Vessel being pushed ahead. Rule 24.

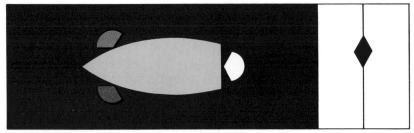

Fig. 19 Vessel being towed astern. Rule 24.

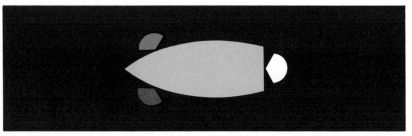

Fig. 20 Vessel being towed alongside. Rule 24.

VESSELS IN TOW

Figure 18

Required lights

Sidelights (112.5°) at forward end
Inland only: special flashing light, yellow (180°–225°)

Notes

Any number of vessels being pushed in a group shall be lighted as one vessel.

When a pushing vessel and a vessel being pushed ahead are rigidly connected in a composite unit they shall be regarded as a power-driven vessel and exhibit the lights prescribed in Rule 23.

Figure 19

Required lights

Sidelights (112.5°)
Sternlight (135°)

Dayshape

Diamond where best seen, when length of tow exceeds 200 meters

Figure 20

Required lights

Sidelights at forward end (112.5°)
Sternlight   (135°)

Note

Any number of vessels being towed alongside in a group shall be lighted as one vessel.

PARTLY SUBMERGED VESSEL OR OBJECT BEING TOWED

Figure 21

Required lights

Less than 25 meters in breadth:
all-round white light at each end.

25 meters or more in breadth:
4 all-round white lights to mark length and breadth.

Greater than 100 meters in length:
additional lights so that the distance between the lights shall not exceed 100 meters.

Dayshape

Diamond at or near the aftermost extremity of the last vessel or object being towed. The COLREGS also require a diamond at the forward end if the length of the tow exceeds 200 meters.

Notes

Vessels or objects towed alongside shall be lighted as one vessel or object.

The towing vessel may direct a searchlight in the direction of the tow to indicate its presence to an approaching vessel.

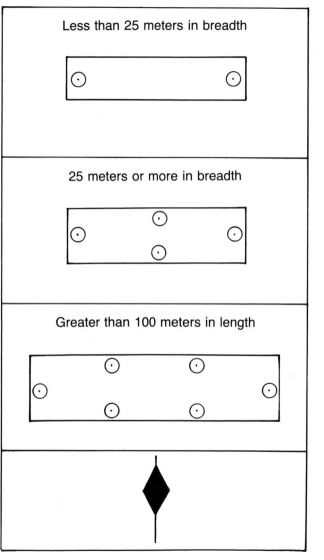

Fig. 21 Partly submerged vessel or object being towed. Inland Rule 24.

Fig. 22 Vessel engaged in fishing—left, at anchor or not making way; right, making way. Rule 26.

Fig. 23 Vessel engaged in trawling—left, at anchor or not making way; right, making way. Rule 26.

FISHING VESSELS

Figure 22

Required lights

Red over white at masthead (all-round)

White light (all-round) required if outlying gear extends more than 150 meters horizontally from vessel. Must be placed to show direction toward the gear (not shown in Figure 22)

Sidelights and sternlight required *only when making way through the water*

Dayshapes

2 cones with apexes together in a vertical line. A vessel less than 20 meters may substitute a basket for these shapes.

Cone apex upward to show direction of outlying gear if gear extends more than 150 meters horizontally from the vessel.

Figure 23

Required lights

Green over white at masthead (all-round)

*Range light (225°) higher than green light when displayed—not shown in Figure 23 (*see* page 10)

Sidelights and sternlight required *only when making way through the water*

Dayshapes

2 cones with apexes together in a vertical line. A vessel of less than 20 meters in length may substitute a basket for these shapes.

VESSELS NOT UNDER COMMAND

Figure 24

Required lights

Red over red (all-round) in vertical line where best seen

Sidelights and sternlight *only if making way through the water*

Dayshapes

2 balls in a vertical line where best seen

Fig. 24 Vessel not under command—left, not making way; right, making way. Rule 27.

VESSELS ENGAGED IN MINESWEEPING

Figure 25

Required lights

3 green lights (all-round), one at foremast head and one at each end of fore yard

Masthead light (225°)

*Range light (225°)—not shown in Figure 25 (*see* page 10)

Sidelights (112.5°)

Sternlight (135°)

Dayshapes

3 balls in same position as the green lights

Inland Note

These lights and shapes indicate that it is dangerous to approach closer than 1,000 meters astern or 500 meters on either side.

COLREG NOTES

These lights and shapes indicate that it is dangerous to approach within 1,000 meters. A vessel engaged in mine clearance operations while at anchor shall show the 3 green lights in addition to anchor light(s) and the 3 balls in addition to the ball showing a vessel at anchor.

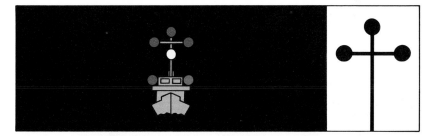

Fig. 25 Vessel engaged in minesweeping. Rule 27.

Fig. 26 Vessel restricted in ability to maneuver (except minesweeping)—left, not making way; right, making way. Rule 27.

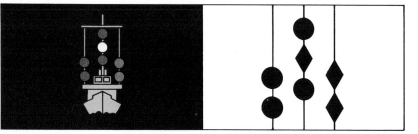

Fig. 27 Vessel engaged in dredging or underwater operations, when restricted in ability to maneuver (when at anchor or not making way). Rule 27.

VESSELS RESTRICTED IN THEIR ABILITY TO MANEUVER

Figure 26

Required lights
Red–white–red (all-round) in a vertical line where best seen
Masthead, *range light (*see* page 10), sidelights and sternlight shown *only if making way through the water*

Dayshapes
Ball–diamond–ball in a vertical line where best seen

Note
When at anchor, red–white–red lights shown *in addition to* anchor lights.

Figure 27

Required lights
Red–white–red (all-round) in a vertical line where best seen
When an obstruction exists:
    obstructed side—red over red (all-round)
    clear side—green over green (all-round)
Masthead light, *range light (*see* page 10), sidelights and sternlight shown *only when making way through the water* (not shown in Figure 27)

Dayshapes
2 balls in a vertical line on obstructed side
Ball–diamond–ball in a vertical line where best seen
2 diamonds in a vertical line on clear side

Figure 28

Dayshape

Rigid replica of the International Code flag "Alpha"

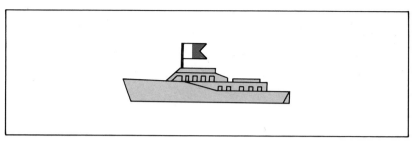

Fig. 28 Diving operations, when size of vessel makes it impracticable to show the shapes in Fig. 27. Rule 27.

PILOT VESSELS

Figure 29

Required lights

White over red (all-round) in a vertical line at or near the masthead
Sidelights (112.5°)
Sternlight (135°)

Fig. 29 Pilot vessel underway. Rule 29.

Figure 30

Required lights

White over red (all-round) in a vertical line at or near the masthead
Anchor lights for a vessel of her length

Dayshape

One ball

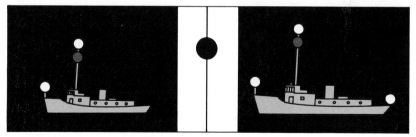

Fig. 30 Pilot vessel at anchor—left, less than 50 meters; right, 50 meters and upward. Rule 29.

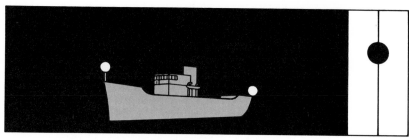

Fig. 31 Vessel at anchor. Rule 30.

VESSELS AT ANCHOR

Figure 31

Required lights

> White light (all-round) in fore part of vessel
> White light (all-round) near the stern and lower than the forward light

Other lights

> A vessel of less than 50 meters in length may substitute one white light (all-round) where best seen

Dayshape

> One ball where best seen

Note

> Vessels of 100 meters and more in length are required to illuminate their decks; optional for smaller vessels.

VESSELS AGROUND

Figure 32

Required lights

> Red over red (all-round) in a vertical line where best seen
> Anchor lights for a vessel of her length

Dayshapes

> 3 balls in a vertical line where best seen

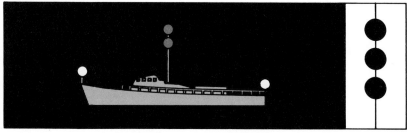

Fig. 32 Vessel aground. Rule 30.

VESSELS CONSTRAINED BY DRAFT (COLREGS ONLY)

Figure 33

Required lights

Normal lights for a power-driven vessel

Other lights

3 red lights (all-round) in a vertical line where best seen, optional

Dayshape

Cylinder where best seen, optional

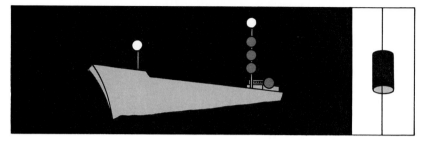

Fig. 33 Vessel constrained by draft. COLREGS Rule 28.

SUMMARY OF IMPORTANT PROVISIONS

A *power-driven vessel* of any length, when underway, is required to show a masthead light, sidelights, and sternlight. The after range light is required for vessels of 50 meters and upward in length, and optional for smaller vessels.

A *power-driven vessel engaged in towing or pushing* displays two towing masthead lights, except when towing astern and the length of the tow exceeds 200 meters, in which case she shows three towing masthead lights. Vessels also have the option of showing two or three towing *range* lights instead of two or three towing *masthead* lights. (In the Inland Rules only, the masthead light is required with the towing range lights.) One yellow towing light is displayed above the sternlight when towing astern. When pushing ahead or towing alongside, the Inland Rules require two yellow towing lights while the COLREGS require only a sternlight. A vessel "engaged in a towing operation such as severely restricts the towing vessel and her tow in their ability to deviate from their course" shows the red–white–red lights in a vertical line *in addition to* the other lights displayed by a towing vessel; she also shows the ball–diamond–ball shapes in the daytime. If towing astern and the length of the tow exceeds 200 meters, a diamond is displayed by both the towing vessel and the tow.

Vessels *engaged in fishing or trawling*, and vessels *not under command* display sidelights and a sternlight only when making way through the water. The special arrays all include two all-round lights: red over white for fishing; green over white for trawling; and red over red for not under command. Other lights include: the white light for a vessel engaged in fishing with gear extending more than 150 meters horizontally from the vessel; and the after range light for the trawler (optional if length of trawler is less than 50 meters). Annex II authorizes additional light signals for fishing vessels fishing in close proximity.

Vessels restricted in their ability to maneuver, except minesweepers and towing vessels, display a masthead light, range light, sidelights, and sternlight only if making way through the water. The special array is the red–white–red lights in a vertical line. A vessel engaged in dredging or underwater operations also shows the two red lights on the obstructed side, and two green lights on the clear side.

A *vessel engaged in minesweeping* shows three green lights or three balls in addition to the lights for a power-driven vessel.

A *vessel constrained by her draft* (COLREGS only) is permitted to show three red lights in a vertical line or a cylinder in addition to the lights for a power-driven vessel.

All *pilot vessels* underway and engaged in pilotage duty show white over red all-round lights in addition to sidelights and a sternlight.

Vessels at anchor are required to show two white all-round lights, with the forward light the higher of the two. A vessel less than 50 meters in length may instead show only one light. In the Inland Rules *only*: "A vessel of less than 20 meters in length, when at anchor in a special anchorage area designated by the Secretary, shall not be required to exhibit the anchor lights and shapes." A vessel restricted in her ability to maneuver, except minesweepers and towing vessels, shows the anchor light(s) or shape *in addition to* the red–white–red lights or ball–diamond–ball shapes. In the COLREGS, a vessel engaged in mine clearance operations shows the anchor light(s) or shape *in addition to* the three green lights or three balls. A pilot vessel shows the white over red lights in addition to the anchor light(s). A vessel engaged in dredging or underwater operations while at anchor shows *only* the red–white–red lights, the two green lights and the two red lights, or the corresponding shapes in the daytime. A fishing vessel does not show anchor lights, being required to show the same lights at anchor that she shows when underway with no way on.

A *vessel aground* shows two all-round lights, red over red, in addition to her anchor light(s), or three balls during the day.

A *vessel proceeding under sail and power* is required to show a cone, point down. A vessel displaying this shape is a "power-driven vessel" for the purpose of the other rules.

Sailing vessels underway have the option of showing red over green (all-round) lights at the masthead in addition to the required sidelights and sternlight.

MISCELLANEOUS PROVISIONS

RULE 37—DISTRESS SIGNALS

When a vessel is in distress and requires assistance she shall use or exhibit the signals prescribed in Annex IV to these Rules:

1. The following signals, used or exhibited either together or separately, indicate distress and need of assistance:
   (a) a gun or other explosive signal fired at intervals of about a minute;
   (b) a continuous sounding with any fog-signalling apparatus;
   (c) rockets or shells, throwing red stars fired one at a time at short intervals;
   (d) a signal made by radiotelegraphy or by any other signalling method consisting of the group ···— — —··· (SOS) in the Morse Code;
   (e) a signal sent by radiotelephony consisting of the spoken word "Mayday";
   (f) the International Code Signal of distress indicated by N.C.;
   (g) a signal consisting of a square flag having above or below it a ball or anything resembling a ball;
   (h) flames on the vessel (as from a burning tar barrel, oil barrel, etc.);
   (i) a rocket parachute flare or a hand flare showing a red light;
   (j) a smoke signal giving off orange-coloured smoke;
   (k) slowly and repeatedly raising and lowering arms outstretched to each side;
   (l) the radiotelegraph alarm signal;
   (m) the radiotelephone alarm signal;
   (n) signals transmitted by emergency position-indicating radio beacons.

2. The use or exhibition of any of the foregoing signals except for the purpose of indicating distress and need of assistance and the use of other signals which may be confused with any of the above signals is prohibited.
3. Attention is drawn to the relevant sections of the International Code of Signals, the Merchant Ship Search and Rescue Manual and the following signals:
   (a) a piece of orange-coloured canvas with either a black square and circle or other appropriate symbol (for identification from the air);
   (b) a dye marker.

Note: Although not specified in the rules, a distress signal that is accepted by custom is an inverted ensign, both in inland and international waters. However, such a signal is not appropriate for use by a man-of-war.

RULE 36—SIGNALS TO ATTRACT ATTENTION

If necessary to attract the attention of another vessel, any vessel may make light or sound signals that cannot be mistaken for any signal authorized elsewhere in these Rules, or may direct the beam of her searchlight in the direction of the danger, in such a way as not to embarrass any vessel.

Note: COLREGS Rule 36 has additional provisions. *See* page 128.

ADDITIONAL STATION LIGHTS, SIGNAL LIGHTS, OR WHISTLE SIGNALS

As authorized by COLREGS Rule 1(c), Inland Rule 1(c) states:

(c) Nothing in these Rules shall interfere with the operation of any special rules made by the Secretary of the Navy with respect to additional station or signal lights and shapes or whistle signals for ships of war and vessels proceeding under convoy, or by the Secretary with respect to additional station or signal lights and shapes for fishing vessels engaged in fishing as a fleet. These additional station or signal lights and shapes or whistle signals shall, so far as possible, be such that they cannot be mistaken for any light, shape, or signal authorized elsewhere under these Rules. Notice of such special rules shall be published in the Federal Register and, after the effective date specified in such notice, they shall have effect as if they were a part of these Rules.

VESSELS OF SPECIAL CONSTRUCTION OR PURPOSE

Under the authority of International Rule 1(e), the United States has passed laws authorizing the Secretary of the Navy and the Secretary of Transportation to exempt Navy and Coast Guard vessels of special construction from certain requirements pertaining to lights.[1] The Coast Guard exceptions are published in Title 33, Code of Federal Regulations. Light waivers for naval vessels are published in Title 32, Code of Federal Regulations. Such exceptions are reproduced in CG-169.

Rule 1(e) of the COLREGS provides:

Whenever the Government concerned shall have determined that a vessel of special construction or purpose cannot comply fully with the provisions of any of these rules with respect to the number, position, range or arc of visibility of lights or shapes, as well as to the disposition and characteristics of sound-signalling appliances, without interfering with the special function of the vessel, such vessel shall comply with such other provisions in regard to the number, position, range or arc of visibility of lights or shapes, as well as to the disposition and characteristics of sound-signalling appliances, as her Government shall have determined to be the closest possible compliance with these rules in respect to that vessel.

SUBMARINES

U.S. naval submarines display an intermittent flashing (yellow) beacon with a sequential operation of one flash per second for 3 seconds, followed by a 3-second off period. The light will be exhibited in addition to the other navigational lights for submarines, and displayed in both inland and international waters. (Part 707 of Title 32, Code of Federal Regulations.)

REDUCED LIGHTING REQUIREMENTS FOR SMALL VESSELS

Several of the rules permit reduced lighting requirements for small vessels. These provisions were not included in the preceding diagrams. Remember that *any* vessel less than 20 meters in length may combine the sidelights in one lantern.

In the COLREGS, a *power-driven vessel* of less than 7 meters in length and whose maximum speed does not exceed 7 knots may show one all-round white light in lieu of all other lights, but such a vessel shall, if practicable, also exhibit sidelights (Rule 23).

---

1. 33 USC 1052 and 33 USC 360.

Both the COLREGS and the Inland Rules permit *power-driven vessels* less than *12 meters* in length (regardless of speed) to show one all-round white light, in lieu of the masthead light and sternlight. For this size vessel, however, the rules require sidelights to be shown (Rule 23).

A *sailing vessel* of less than 7 meters in length shall, if practicable, exhibit sidelights and a sternlight, *or* a single lantern at or near the top of the mast combining sidelights and a sternlight. If she does not, she shall have at hand a white light to show in sufficient time to prevent collision (Rule 25).

A *vessel under oars* may exhibit sidelights and a sternlight, but if she does not, she shall have at hand a white light to show in sufficient time to prevent collision (Rule 25).

For *vessels not under command or restricted in their ability to maneuver*, both the COLREGS and the Inland Rules exempt vessels of less than 12 meters in length from the lights required in Rule 27, but a small vessel engaged in diving operations must at least show red–white–red; she is exempted from the other lights consisting of two red lights on the obstructed side and two green lights on the clear side. Both the COLREGS and the Inland rules also exempt vessels less than 12 meters in length, except when engaged in diving operations, from the *shapes* required in Rule 27.

A vessel of less than 7 meters in length, when *at anchor or aground*, not in or near a narrow channel, fairway, or anchorage, or where other vessels normally navigate, is not required to exhibit anchor lights or shapes (Rule 30). Both the COLREGS and the Inland Rules also exempt ves-sels less than 12 meters in length from the requirement for a vessel aground to show two all-round red lights or three balls (Rule 30).

ADDITIONAL PROVISIONS FOR LIGHTS AND SHAPES IN INLAND WATERS— ANNEX V, PILOT RULES[2]

§88.09 TEMPORARY EXEMPTION FROM LIGHT AND SHAPE REQUIREMENTS WHEN OPERATING UNDER BRIDGES.

A vessel may lower its lights and shapes if necessary to pass under a bridge.

§88.11 LAW ENFORCEMENT VESSELS.

(a) Law enforcement vessels may display a flashing blue light when engaged in direct law enforcement activities. This light shall be located so that it does not interfere with the visibility of the vessel's navigation lights.

(b) The blue light described in this section may be displayed by law enforcement vessels of the United States and the States and their political subdivisions.

§88.13 LIGHTS ON BARGES AT BANK OR DOCK

(a) The following barges shall display at night and in periods of restricted visibility the lights described in paragraph (b) of this section—

2. The following section is a proposed draft at time of this writing.

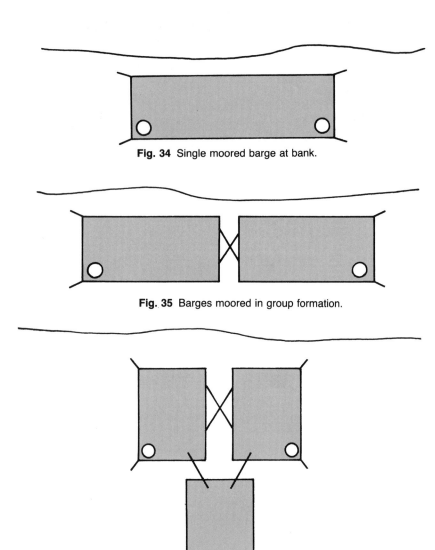

Fig. 34 Single moored barge at bank.

Fig. 35 Barges moored in group formation.

Fig. 36 Barge projecting from a group.

(1) Every barge projecting into a buoyed or restricted channel.

(2) Every barge so moored that it reduces the available navigable width of any channel to less than 80 meters.

(3) Barges moored in fleets more than two barges wide or to a maximum width of over 25 meters.

(4) Every barge not moored parallel to the bank.

(b) Barges described in paragraph (a) shall carry two unobstructed white lights of an intensity to be visible for at least one mile on a clear dark night, and arranged as follows.

(1) On a single moored barge, lights shall be placed on the two corners farthest from the bank [Figure 34].

(2) On barges moored in group formation, a light shall be placed on each of the upstream and downstream ends of the group, on the corners farthest from the bank [Figure 35].

(3) Any barge in a group, but projecting from it toward the channel, shall be lighted as a single barge [Figure 36].

(c) Barges moored in any slip or slough which is used primarily for mooring purposes are exempt from the lighting requirements of this section.

(d) Barges moored in well-illuminated designated areas on United States inland waters are not required to display the lights prescribed in paragraph (b). Each Coast Guard District Commander will publish a list of such designated areas.

§88.15 LIGHTS ON DREDGE PIPELINES [FIGURE 37]

Dredge pipelines that are floating or supported on trestles shall display the following lights at night and in periods of restricted visibility.

(a) One row of yellow lights. The lights must be—
   (1) Flashing 50 to 70 times per minute,
   (2) Visible all around the horizon,
   (3) Not less than 2 and not more than 3.5 meters above the water,
   (4) Approximately equally spaced, and
   (5) Not more than 10 meters apart where the pipeline crosses a navigable channel. Where the pipeline does not cross a navigable channel the lights must be sufficient in number to clearly show the pipeline's length and course.

(b) Two red lights at each end of the pipeline. The lights must be—
   (1) Visible all around the horizon, and
   (2) One meter apart in a vertical line with the lower light at the same height above the water as the flashing yellow light.

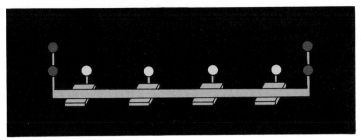

Fig. 37 Lights on dredge pipelines.

3 Right of Way and Signals for All Vessels

This chapter is concerned with right of way provisions *other than* those which apply only to a power-driven vessel approaching another power-driven vessel, and it outlines signals that *all* vessels must use. Right of way provisions and signals that apply only to power-driven vessels will be discussed in chapters 4 through 7.

Whenever two vessels are approaching each other, at least one of them is required to keep out of the way of the other. A vessel required to maneuver is called the *give-way* vessel, and may be required to change course, change speed, or both, in order to keep out of the way of the other vessel. (The term formerly used in the rules for give-way vessel was burdened vessel.) In some situations, both vessels are required to give way. The excerpts from Rules 16 and 8 which detail the duties of the give-way vessel are the same in the COLREGS and Inland Rules:

Rule 16—Action by Give-Way Vessel
Every vessel which is directed to keep out of the way of another vessel shall, so far as possible, take early and substantial action to keep well clear.

Rule 8—Action to Avoid Collision
(a) Any action taken to avoid collision shall, if the circumstances of the case admit, be positive, made in ample time and with due regard to the observance of good seamanship.
(b) Any alteration of course or speed to avoid collision shall, if the circumstances of the case admit, be large enough to be readily apparent to another vessel observing visually or by radar; a succession of small alterations of course or speed should be avoided.
(c) If there is sufficient sea room, alteration of course alone may be the most effective action to avoid a close-quarters situation provided that it is made in good time, is substantial and does not result in another close-quarters situation.
(d) Action taken to avoid collision with another vessel shall be such as to result in passing at a safe distance. The effectiveness of the action

shall be carefully checked until the other vessel is finally past and clear.

If two vessels are approaching in a situation such that only one is a give-way vessel, the other is the *stand-on* vessel. (The term formerly used in the rules for stand-on vessel was privileged vessel.) The duties of the stand-on vessel are given in the following excerpt from Rule 17 (COLREGS and Inland):

> (a) (i) Where one of two vessels is to keep out of the way, the other shall keep her course and speed.
>
> (ii) The latter vessel may, however, take action to avoid collision by her maneuver alone, as soon as it becomes apparent to her that the vessel required to keep out of the way is not taking appropriate action in compliance with these Rules.
>
> (b) When, from any cause, the vessel required to keep her course and speed finds herself so close that collision cannot be avoided by the action of the give-way vessel alone, she shall take such action as will best aid to avoid collision. . . .
>
> (d) This Rule does not relieve the give-way vessel of her obligation to keep out of the way.

RIGHT OF WAY

The following right of way topics are listed in the order of their precedence. The right of way provisions for a sailing vessel approaching another sailing vessel are also covered at the end of this section.

Approaching a vessel which is not underway
Overtaking
Narrow channels and traffic separation schemes
Right of way between different categories of vessels

APPROACHING A VESSEL WHICH IS NOT UNDERWAY

The presumption of fault will be against a moving vessel in cases where a moving vessel collides with a vessel that is not underway (or with a vessel that is underway and not moving). In some cases, however, the vessel not underway may be found at fault for improper lights or for improper position. The circumstances may dictate that a vessel at anchor must have an anchor watch to give some warning in addition to the anchor lights, or to protect against the possibility of dragging. In one court case, a vessel anchored in fog was found liable for 20 percent of incurred damages for her failure to keep her engines on standby and to let go the anchor chain to avoid collision. These precautions were necessary because the traffic and fog made the situation particularly hazardous and the vessel was not anchored in a charted anchorage area.[1]

A typical court opinion in a 1962 case stated:

> Where a moving vessel collides with an anchored vessel, burden is upon moving vessel to exonerate herself from the blame by showing that it was not within her power to have avoided the collision by taking reasonable precautions, but such burden shifts where it appears that a contributing cause of collision was absence of statutory lights on the anchored vessel.[2]

OVERTAKING

Any vessel overtaking any other shall keep out of the way of the vessel being overtaken. A vessel

1. *Getty Oil Co., Inc.* v. *S.S. Ponce De Leon*, C.A.N.Y. 1977, 555 F. 2d 328.
2. *Willis* v. *Tugs Tramp and Mars*, D.C. Va. 1962, 216 F. Supp. 901.

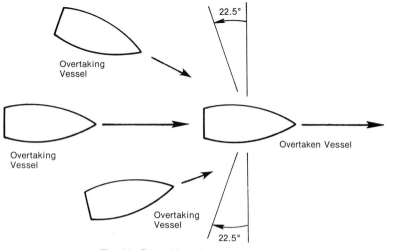

Fig. 38 Overtaking situation.

is overtaking if she approaches the vessel ahead from more than 22.5 degrees abaft her beam (*see* Figure 38). If there is any doubt that a vessel is forward or abaft this direction from the vessel ahead, she shall assume that she is overtaking. At night a vessel overtaking another would be unable to see either sidelight of the vessel ahead.

NARROW CHANNELS AND TRAFFIC SEPARATION SCHEMES

Traffic separation schemes are set up offshore for controlling areas where there is heavy traffic. Right of way in narrow channels differs primarily in that larger vessels cannot leave the channel because of draft limitations. In addition, certain locations have a vessel traffic service, and Inland Rule 10 requires vessels to comply with its regulations.

Right of way in narrow channels is governed by the following excerpt from Rule 9 (COLREGS and Inland Rules):

A vessel of less than 20 meters in length or a sailing vessel shall[3] not impede the passage of a vessel which can safely navigate only within a narrow channel or fairway.

A vessel engaged in fishing shall not impede the passage of any other vessel navigating within a narrow channel or fairway.

A vessel shall not cross a narrow channel or fairway if such crossing impedes the passage of a vessel which can safely navigate only within such channel or fairway. The latter vessel shall use the danger signal prescribed in Rule 34(d) if in doubt as to the intention of the crossing vessel.

3. "Shall" is used in the Inland Rules and "may" is used in the COLREGS.

Rule 9 also requires: "A vessel proceeding along the course of a narrow channel or fairway shall keep as near to the outer limit of the channel or fairway which lies on her starboard side as is safe and practicable"; and "Every vessel shall, if the circumstances of the case admit, avoid anchoring in a narrow channel."

All vessels less than 20 meters in length, sailing vessels, and vessels engaged in fishing shall not impede the passage of a vessel which can safely navigate only within a narrow channel or fairway. Such a large vessel should alert a small vessel of her duty with the danger signal if it appears that the smaller vessel will get in the way. An overtaken vessel is still the stand-on vessel, and a large vessel must be prepared to slow down to the speed of the vessel ahead until the smaller vessel has an opportunity to get out of the way. Small vessels must also be alert to the danger posed by large power-driven vessels who may travel a great distance before a backing bell effectively reduces their headway.

The following excerpt from COLREGS Rule 10 (*see* Figure 39) gives the general provisions for a traffic separation scheme adopted by IMCO (Intergovernmental Maritime Consultative Organization):

   (a) This rule applies to traffic separation schemes adopted by the organization [IMCO].

   (b) A vessel using a traffic separation scheme shall:

      (i) proceed in the appropriate traffic lane in the general direction of traffic flow for that lane [vessel A];

     (ii) so far as practicable, keep clear of a traffic separation line or separation zone [vessel B];

    (iii) normally join or leave a traffic lane at the termination of the lane [vessel C], but

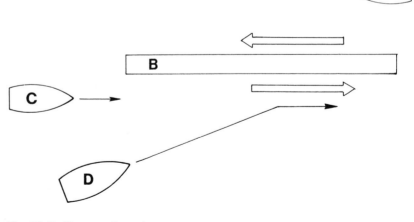

Fig. 39 Traffic-separation schemes.

when joining or leaving from either side shall do so at as small an angle to the general direction of traffic flow as practicable [vessel D].

(d) Inshore traffic zones shall not normally be used by through traffic which can safely use the appropriate traffic lane within the adjacent traffic separation scheme. However, vessels less than 20 meters in length and sailing vessels may under all circumstances use inshore traffic zones.

(e) A vessel, other than a crossing vessel or a vessel joining or leaving a lane, shall not normally enter a separation zone or cross a separation line except:

    (i) in cases of emergency to avoid immediate danger;

    (ii) to engage in fishing within a separation zone.

(f) A vessel navigating in areas near the terminations of traffic separation schemes shall do so with particular caution.

(g) A vessel shall so far as practicable avoid anchoring in a traffic separation scheme or in areas near its terminations.

Right of way in traffic separation schemes is governed by the following excerpt from COLREGS Rule 10:

A vessel of less than 20 metres in length or a sailing vessel shall not impede the safe passage of a power-driven vessel following a traffic lane.

A vessel engaged in fishing shall not impede the passage of any vessel following a traffic lane.

A vessel not using a traffic separation scheme shall avoid it by as wide a margin as is practicable.

A vessel shall so far as practicable avoid crossing traffic lanes, but if obliged to so do shall cross as nearly as practicable at right angles to the general direction of traffic flow.

RIGHT OF WAY BETWEEN DIFFERENT CATEGORIES OF VESSELS

Rule 18 provides a hierarchy of "responsibilities between vessels." Except where Rule 9 (Narrow Channels), Rule 10 (Traffic Separation Schemes or Vessel Traffic Services), or Rule 13 (Overtaking) otherwise require, all vessels underway shall keep out of the way of vessels in all categories which are listed *below* the category pertaining to their own vessel:

CATEGORY	SPECIAL LIGHT ARRAY
1. Power-driven vessel	None
Pilot vessel	White over red
Towing vessel	Towing masthead (or range) lights
2. Sailing vessel	Red over green (optional)
3. Engaged in fishing	Red over white
Engaged in trawling	Green over white
4. Not under command and	Red over red
Restricted in ability to maneuver	Red–white–red
Minesweeping	3 green lights

The COLREGS have an additional provision in Rule 18 not found in the Inland Rules:

(d)(i) Any vessel other than a vessel not under command or a vessel restricted in her ability to manoeuvre shall, if the circumstances of the case admit, avoid impeding the safe passage of a vessel constrained by her draught, exhibiting the signals in Rule 28 [three red lights in a vertical line or a cylinder].

(ii) A vessel constrained by her draught shall navigate with particular caution having full regard to her special condition.

RIGHT OF WAY— SAILING VESSEL APPROACHING SAILING VESSEL

Rule 12—Sailing Vessels (COLREGS and Inland Rules)

(a) When two sailing vessels are approaching one another, so as to involve risk of collision, one of them shall keep out of the way of the other as follows:

(i) When each has the wind on a different side, the vessel which has the wind on the port side shall keep out of the way of the other.

(ii) When both have the wind on the same side, the vessel which is to windward shall keep out of the way of the vessel which is to leeward.

(iii) If a vessel with the wind on the port side sees a vessel to windward and cannot determine with certainty whether the other vessel has the wind on the port or on the starboard side, she shall keep out of the way of the other.

(b) For the purpose of this Rule the windward side shall be deemed to be the side opposite to that on which the mainsail is carried or, in the case of a square-rigged vessel, the side opposite to that on which the largest fore-and-aft sail is carried.

SIGNALS FOR ALL VESSELS

DANGER SIGNAL (Rule 34(d), COLREGS and Inland Rules)

When vessels[4] in sight of one another are approaching each other and from any cause either vessel fails to understand the intentions or actions of the other, or is in doubt whether sufficient action is being taken by the other to avoid collision, the vessel in doubt shall immediately indicate such doubt by giving at least five short and rapid blasts on the whistle. Such signal may be supplemented by a light signal of at least five short and rapid flashes.

BEND SIGNAL (Rule 34(e), COLREGS and Inland Rules)

A vessel[4] nearing a bend or an area of a channel or fairway where other vessels may be obscured by an intervening obstruction shall sound one prolonged blast. Such signal shall be answered with a prolonged blast by any approaching vessel that may be within hearing around the bend or behind the intervening obstruction.

COLREGS SIGNALS FOR OVERTAKING IN RESTRICTED WATERS

In the Inland Rules, signals are sounded in the overtaking situation only if *both* vessels are power-driven vessels. In the COLREGS, the signals required and the conduct of the vessels during passing depends upon the geographic characteristics of the area. In open waters, only power-driven vessels sound signals when overtaking other vessels. Chapter 5 deals with the subject of the over-

4. "Vessel" includes every description of watercraft (Rule 3).

taking situation for power-driven vessels. When *not* in open waters, but in "a narrow channel or fairway when overtaking can take place only if the vessel to be overtaken has to take action to permit safe passing," the COLREGS require *all vessels* to exchange signals of intent-agreement. The vessel intending to overtake shall indicate her intention by sounding the following signals on her whistle:

—two prolonged blasts followed by one short blast to mean "I intend to overtake you on your starboard side";
—two prolonged blasts followed by two short blasts to mean "I intend to overtake you on your port side." [Rule 34(c)]

The vessel to be overtaken shall, if in agreement, sound the following signal on her whistle: one prolonged, one short, one prolonged, and one short, in that order (International Code group "Charlie" meaning "affirmative"). The overtaken vessel shall then take steps to permit safe passing.

If the overtaken vessel is not in agreement, she may sound instead the danger signal of five or more short blasts. The overtaking vessel should not attempt passing until an agreement is reached, nor does agreement relieve her of her obligation to keep out of the way until well past and clear.

EQUIPMENT FOR SOUND SIGNALS

Rule 33, Equipment for Sound Signals, requires that *all vessels* of 12 meters or more in length have a whistle and a bell complying with the specifications in Annex III (all vessels of 100 meters or more in length are required to have a gong). Vessels less than 12 meters in length are not required to have a whistle and bell which comply with Annex III, but if they do not, they must "be provided with some other means of making an efficient sound signal." Annex III requires lower frequency whistles for large vessels (based on length) and higher frequencies for smaller vessels.

4 Introduction to Approach Situations for Power-Driven Vessels

Chapter 3 discussed the right of way between various categories of vessels as well as the right of way between two sailing vessels. For power-driven vessels approaching each other, however, the stand-on or give-way status is determined by the approach situation—overtaking, meeting, or crossing. Two conditions are necessary before any of the three approach situations can exist between two power-driven vessels:

1. There must be a risk of collision.
2. The vessels must be in sight of each other.

RISK OF COLLISION

Rule 7 of both the COLREGS and the Inland Rules states:

> (d) In determining if risk of collision exists the following considerations shall be among those taken into account:
> (i) such risk shall be deemed to exist if the compass bearing of an approaching vessel does not appreciably change; and

> (ii) such risk may sometimes exist even when an appreciable bearing change is evident, particularly when approaching a very large vessel or a tow or when approaching a vessel at close range.

There can be no hard-and-fast rule which prescribes a rate-of-bearing change by which risk of collision can be determined. Bearings will change at different rates for vessels at different ranges from each other. The one conclusion that can be made is that taking bearings on an approaching vessel is a requirement of the rules. It is important that the bearings be compass bearings (true or magnetic), since relative bearings provide no useful information when heading is changed. If the true bearing of a vessel remains nearly constant, and the range is decreasing, the two vessels are on a collision course. When the true bearings are changing rapidly, the bearings will show the side on which the other vessel will pass, providing both vessels maintain course and speed. If the bearing is increasing numerically, a vessel on the starboard hand will pass astern, a vessel on the port hand will cross ahead. If the bearing is decreasing numerically, a vessel on the starboard hand will cross ahead, a vessel on the port hand will pass astern.

The meaning of *risk of collision* has been expanded by the courts:

> Risk of collision begins the very moment when the two vessels have approached so near each other and upon such courses, that by a departure from the rules of navigation, whether from want of good seamanship, accident, mistake, misapprehension of signals, or otherwise, a collision might be brought about. It is true, that, prima facie, each has a right to assume that the other will obey the law. But this does not justify either in shutting his eyes to what the other may actually do, or in omitting to do what he can to avoid an accident, made imminent by the acts of the other. I say the right above is prima facie merely because it is known that departures from the law not only may, but do, take place, and often. Risk of collision may be said to begin the moment the two vessels have approached so near that a collision might be brought about by any such departure, and continues up to the moment when they have so far progressed that no such result could ensue. . . . The idea that there was no risk of collision is fully exploded by the fact that there was a collision.[1]

VESSELS IN SIGHT

The meeting, overtaking, and crossing situations apply only to vessels in sight (this does not include tracking by radar). The situations apply in fog and other conditions of restricted visibility, *but only after the vessels have sighted each other.*

1. The *Milwaukee*, 1871, Fed. Cas. No. 9, 626.

PROVISIONS FOR INLAND WATERS ONLY

POWER-DRIVEN VESSEL LEAVING A DOCK OR BERTH (INLAND RULES ONLY)

Rule 34(g) of the Inland Rules requires the following:
"When a power-driven vessel is leaving a dock or berth, she shall sound one prolonged blast." This signal is required even though the vessel moving from her dock or berth is in sight of other vessels.[2] The courts have ruled that a vessel moving from her dock or berth is in "special circumstances" until settled on her course. This situation will be elaborated in Chapter 9.

VESSEL BRIDGE-TO-BRIDGE RADIOTELEPHONE ACT (INLAND WATERS ONLY)

This law went into effect on 1 January 1973, and is an important step toward the prevention of collisions in inland waters (it also applies to the Great Lakes and Western Rivers). It requires the following vessels to guard the frequency 156.65 MHz for bridge-to-bridge communications:

1. Power-driven vessels of 300 gross tons and upward.
2. Vessels of 100 gross tons and upward that are for hire and carry one or more passengers.
3. Commercial towing vessels of 26 feet or over in length.
4. Manned dredges and floating plants working in or near a channel or fairway.

2. *Grace Line, Inc.* v. *U.S. Lines Co.*, D.C.N.Y. 1961, 193 F. Supp. 664.

The radiotelephone frequency is for the exclusive use of the person in charge of the vessel, who shall, when necessary, *transmit and confirm the intentions of his vessel and any other information necessary for the safe navigation of vessels.* Even when not transmitting, guarding the frequency can be invaluable in appraising a traffic situation; knowledge of the intentions of other vessels is added to what is ordinarily observed by radar or visual means, or by the signals of vessels within range of hearing.

The primary advantage of the bridge-to-bridge radiotelephone is gained when communication between two vessels results in agreement on their intentions in a situation which might have ended in collision because of misunderstanding and confusion. In the following discussion on the three approach situations, keep in mind that signals are not always heard, and are often misinterpreted when only part of the signal is heard (example: one blast heard when two were sounded). This writer recommends that whenever the course or intention of another vessel is not *immediately* understood, communication should be established on the bridge-to-bridge frequency. In this way, intentions may be confirmed early, and the misunderstandings which would require the sounding of the danger signal would be avoided. Regardless of the information exchanged, nothing in the Radiotelephone Act "relieves any person from the obligation of complying with the rules of the road and applicable pilot rules." The following provision is from Inland Rule 34(h):

A vessel that reaches agreement with another vessel in a meeting, crossing, or overtaking situation by using the radiotelephone as prescribed by the Bridge-to-Bridge Radiotelephone Act (85 Stat. 165; 33 U.S.C. 1207), is not obliged to sound the whistle signals prescribed by this Rule, but may do so. If agreement is not reached, then whistle signals shall be exchanged in a timely manner and shall prevail.

Section 83.251 of the regulations issued by the Federal Communications Commission requires transmissions similar to the following format:

THIS IS THE (name of vessel). MY POSITION IS (give readily identifiable position and, if useful, course and speed) ABOUT TO (describe contemplated action). OUT.

VESSEL OFF (give a readily identifiable position). THIS IS (name of vessel) OFF (give a readily identifiable position). I PLAN TO (give proposed course of action). OVER.

Vessels acknowledging receipt shall answer:

(Name of vessel calling). THIS IS (name of vessel answering). RECEIVED YOUR CALL (follow with an indication of intentions). Communications shall terminate when each ship is satisfied that the other no longer poses a threat to its safety and is ended with "OUT."

See Appendix A for log-keeping requirements.

5 Overtaking Situation for Power-Driven Vessels[1]

INLAND SIGNALS FOR OVERTAKING

In the Inland Rules, signals are sounded in the overtaking situation only if *both* vessels are power-driven vessels. The COLREGS signals for overtaking will be covered separately because they are *not* the same. The Inland signals are signals of intent-agreement and are found in Rule 34:

(c) When in sight of one another:
  (i) a power-driven vessel intending to overtake another power-driven vessel shall indicate her intention by the following signals on her whistle: one short blast to mean "I intend to overtake you on your starboard side"; two short blasts to mean "I intend to overtake you on your port side"; and
  (ii) the power-driven vessel about to be overtaken shall, if in agreement, sound a similar sound signal. If in doubt she shall sound the danger signal prescribed in paragraph (d).

The overtaking vessel is the give-way vessel. If she desires to overtake on the starboard side of the vessel ahead she sounds one short blast. If she desires to overtake on the port side of the vessel ahead, she sounds two short blasts.

The overtaken vessel is the stand-on vessel. If she agrees to the signal of the overtaking vessel she answers with the same signal. If she does not agree to the signal—because of an obvious danger ahead or her own plans to make a maneuver—she must immediately answer with the danger signal: five short and rapid blasts on the whistle which may be supplemented by a light signal of five short and rapid flashes. All vessels are forbidden to use what has become known among mariners as "cross signals," that is, answering one whistle with two, and answering two whistles with one. The following paragraph outlines several court requirements governing the overtaking situation.

1. *See* Chapter 3, pp. 33-34 for definition of overtaking situation.

The overtaking vessel is not permitted to pass the vessel ahead until the overtaken vessel answers with the same signal. The overtaken vessel is not obligated to maintain course and speed until she agrees to the signal of the overtaking vessel.[2] The overtaken vessel is legally maintaining course and speed when maneuvering to follow the turns of a channel or to avoid immediate dangers such as rocks or shoals. Such maneuvers must be anticipated by the overtaking vessel. The overtaken vessel may ease to give the passing vessel more room, but she is not required to do so. The courts have generally ruled that the overtaking vessel must signal if she will approach the vessel ahead so close that a sudden change of course by the latter would bring about a collision.

When the first signal of the overtaking vessel is answered with the danger signal, the overtaken vessel can subsequently indicate by one or two short blasts when it is safe to pass, or the overtaking vessel can initiate a new signal of intent. "The signal of an overtaking vessel must be repeated if not responded to, and the possibility of collision avoided, if necessary, by slackening speed and changing course."[3]

A common cause of collisions in the overtaking situation is the suction which draws two ships together. The force of suction is greatest when the overtaking vessel is passing at a high relative speed in shallow water, and particularly when the overtaken vessel is close aboard a deep-draft vessel on one side and a bank on the other.

Remember that discussions in this chapter relate strictly to situations where one power-driven vessel is approaching another power-driven vessel: if one of the two vessels in an overtaking situation is a sailing vessel, no signals will be exchanged.

COLREGS SIGNALS FOR OVERTAKING

The following excerpt from Rule 34, Maneuvering and Warning Signals, of the COLREGS gives the meaning of the one, two, and three short blast signals. The meaning is the same in all of the approach situations—overtaking, meeting, or crossing.

(a) When vessels are in sight of one another, a power-driven vessel underway, when manoeuvering as authorized or required by these rules, shall indicate that manoeuvre by the following signals on her whistle:
—one short blast to mean "I am altering my course to starboard";
—two short blasts to mean "I am altering my course to port";
—three short blasts to mean "I am operating astern propulsion."

(b) Any vessel may supplement the whistle signals prescribed in paragraph (a) of this rule by light signals, repeated as appropriate, whilst the manoeuvre is being carried out.

(i) these light signals shall have the following significance:
—one flash to mean "I am altering my course to starboard";
—two flashes to mean "I am altering my course to port";
—three flashes to mean "I am operating astern propulsion";

(ii) the duration of each flash shall be about one second, the interval be-

2. The *Industry*, C.C.A.N.Y. 1928, 29 F. 2d 29.
3. *Ervin* v. *Neversink Steamboat Co.*, 1882, 88 N.Y. 184.

tween flashes shall be about one second, and the interval between successive signals shall be not less than ten seconds;

(iii) the light used for this signal shall, if fitted, be an all-round white light, visible at a minimum range of 5 miles, and shall comply with the provisions of Annex I to these Regulations.

The one- and two-short-blast signals are required to be given only by power-driven vessels, when a vessel of any type or category is in sight. They are rudder-action signals, intended to inform other vessels that a change of course is being executed. The signal requires no answer from other vessels.

The backing signal of three short blasts is required to be given only by power-driven vessels, when a vessel of any type or category is in sight.

The light signals which can supplement the one-, two-, or three-short-blast signals are optional.

The signals required and the conduct of vessels during the passing depends upon the geographic characteristics of the area.

OVERTAKING SITUATION IN OPEN WATERS

In open waters, the overtaken vessel is the stand-on vessel and is required to maintain course and speed. She is not required to sound any signals, unless she doubts that the give-way vessel is taking sufficient action to avoid collision, in which case she sounds the danger signal of five or more short blasts.

The overtaking vessel is the give-way vessel and is required to keep out of the way until well past

and clear. As she maneuvers to keep clear of the overtaken vessel, she sounds the appropriate signals: one short blast if she turns right; two short blasts if she turns left. If she does not alter course during the passing, no signals will be sounded. Each maneuver should be accompanied by signals as long as the overtaken vessel is in sight (*see* Figure 41).

OVERTAKING SITUATION IN RESTRICTED WATERS

"In a narrow channel or fairway when overtaking can take place only if the vessel to be overtaken has to take action to permit safe passing, the vessel intending to overtake shall indicate her intention by sounding" the following signals on her whistle:

—two prolonged blasts followed by one short blast to mean "I intend to overtake you on your starboard side";

—two prolonged blasts followed by two short blasts to mean "I intend to overtake you on your port side."

The vessel to be overtaken shall, if in agreement, sound the following signal on her whistle: one prolonged, one short, one prolonged, and one short, in that order (International Code group "Charlie" meaning "affirmative"). The overtaken vessel shall then take steps to permit safe passing.

If the overtaken vessel is not in agreement, she may sound instead the danger signal of five or more short blasts. The overtaking vessel should not attempt passing until an agreement is reached, nor does agreement relieve her of her obligation to keep out of the way until well past and clear.

SUMMARY OF OVERTAKING SIGNALS

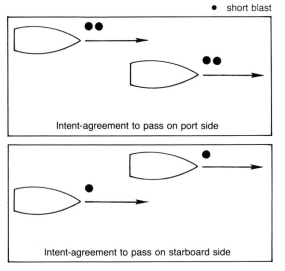

• short blast

Intent-agreement to pass on port side

Intent-agreement to pass on starboard side

Fig. 40 Inland signals of intent-agreement.

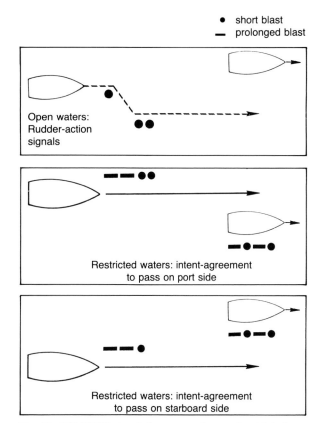

• short blast
— prolonged blast

Open waters:
Rudder-action
signals

Restricted waters: intent-agreement
to pass on port side

Restricted waters: intent-agreement
to pass on starboard side

Fig. 41 COLREGS signals for open waters and restricted waters.

6 Meeting Situation for Power-Driven Vessels

HEAD-ON SITUATION DEFINED

The definition of a head-on situation is the same in the COLREGS and in the Inland Rules.

Rule 14—Head-on Situation

(a) When two power-driven vessels are meeting on reciprocal or nearly reciprocal courses so as to involve risk of collision each shall alter her course to starboard so that each shall pass on the port side of the other.

(b) Such a situation shall be deemed to exist when a vessel sees the other ahead or nearly ahead and by night she could see the masthead lights of the other in a line or nearly in a line or both sidelights and by day she observes the corresponding aspect of the other vessel.

(c) When a vessel is in any doubt as to whether such a situation exists she shall assume that it does exist and act accordingly.

In a head-on situation *both* vessels are give-way vessels and both are required to alter course to starboard in order to pass port to port. A guideline for determining if a head-on situation exists is to consider an approaching vessel "nearly ahead" if she is within one point (11.25 degrees) of the bow—but if there is any doubt, assume that it is a head-on situation. The head-on approach is shown in Figure 42 as Situation 1.

INLAND SIGNALS FOR MEETING

The Inland signals of intent-agreement are found in Rule 34; the corresponding light signals are optional.

Rule 34—Maneuvering and Warning Signals

(a) When power-driven vessels are in sight of one another and meeting or crossing at a distance within half a mile of each other, each vessel underway, when maneuvering as authorized or required by these Rules:

(i) shall indicate that maneuver by the following signals on her whistle: one short blast to mean "I intend to leave you on my port side"; two short blasts to mean

"I intend to leave you on my starboard side"; and three short blasts to mean "I am operating astern propulsion."

  (ii) upon hearing the one or two blast signal of the other shall, if in agreement, sound the same whistle signal and take the steps necessary to effect a safe passing. If, however, from any cause, the vessel doubts the safety of the proposed maneuver, she shall sound the danger signal specified in paragraph (d) of this Rule and each vessel shall take appropriate precautionary action until a safe passing agreement is made.

(b) A vessel may supplement the whistle signals prescribed in paragraph (a) of this Rule by light signals:

  (i) These signals shall have the following significance: one flash to mean "I intend to leave you on my port side"; two flashes to mean "I intend to leave you on my starboard side"; three flashes to mean "I am operating astern propulsion";

  (ii) The duration of each flash shall be about 1 second; and

  (iii) The light used for this signal shall, if fitted, be one all-round white or yellow light, visible at a minimum range of 2 miles, synchronized with the whistle, and shall comply with the provisions of Annex I to these Rules.

When meeting head-on, both vessels are give-way vessels. One vessel proposes a port-to-port passage by sounding one short blast. The other vessel should answer promptly with one short blast, and both are required to alter course to starboard in order to pass port to port. This is the

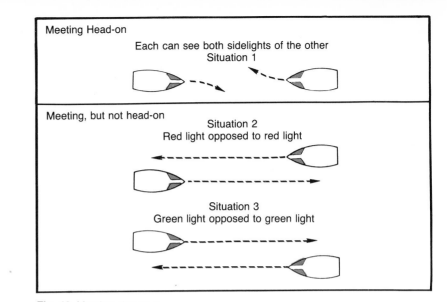

Fig. 42 Meeting situations.

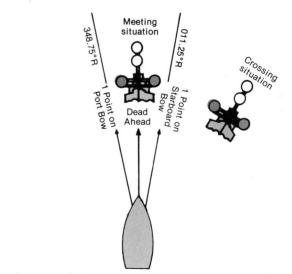

Fig. 43 Crossing v. meeting.

procedure required whenever the vessels cannot pass safely without altering course, even if they are slightly starboard of each other.

While not specifically mentioned in the rules, it is possible that two vessels in a meeting situation could pass within half a mile of each other without being within the definition of a head-on situation. Rule 34 would require that the vessels exchange signals. Without question, the correct procedure for vessels passing port to port is to exchange one-blast signals if they will pass within half a mile, even though no course change is required by either vessel (Situation 2 in Figure 42).

The only place in the rules where a vessel is specifically "authorized or required" to leave the other vessel to starboard is in Rule 9(a)(ii). This provision pertains to a vessel on the Great Lakes or Western Rivers (or waters specified by the Secretary) proceeding with a following current. That vessel has the option of proposing a starboard-to-starboard passage if the current patterns so determine when it is rounding a bend.

Other than the provision discussed in the preceding paragraph, the rules provide no guidance on passing starboard to starboard in a meeting situation (Situation 3 in Figure 42). The following facts apply:

1. If there is no risk of collision, there cannot be a meeting situation, and a starboard-to-starboard passing is proper. However, after a collision it is difficult to argue in court that there was no risk of collision.
2. The *old* Inland Rules *required* vessels to pass starboard to starboard if "so far to the starboard of each other as not to be considered as meeting head and head." The requirements of the old rules do *not* apply now, but

it *is* sometimes safer to pass starboard to starboard than to force a port-to-port passing.
3. The rules definitely require that you assume that a head-on situation exists if you have any doubt. Neither the rules nor past court decisions provide a precise definition of "nearly ahead." A good rule of thumb has been to consider a vessel within a point (11.25 degrees) of your bow to be nearly ahead—this fits most court decisions but cannot be expected to be appropriate to the circumstances of every case.
4. The rules require that signals be exchanged if vessels pass within half a mile.

In order to be qualified as an Officer of the Deck (Underway) or Captain on a Navy or Coast Guard vessel, or licensed as a Mate or Master, an individual must demonstrate an ability to exercise educated judgment. This writer presents the following guidance based on the reading of a great number of court cases and a "feel" for how the courts will rule. Taking into account the prevailing circumstances and conditions:

1. If there is any doubt that a head-on situation exists—pass port to port.
2. If only the green sidelight of a vessel ahead is visible when initially sighted, that is a legal reason to consider the situation *not* within the definition of meeting head-on. A starboard-to-starboard passing would then be appropriate (except in some cases involving winding or turning channels).
3. If a change of course is necessary in order to pass safely, consider the situation to be head-on and pass port to port.
4. If the situation is clearly not head-on and the

vessels can pass starboard to starboard safely with no course change, a starboard-to-starboard passage is appropriate. Judgment is critical here—if there appears to be a danger of collision, a port-to-port passage may be indicated.

5. Use the bridge-to-bridge radiotelephone frequency. *Early* communication saves confusion.

MANEUVERING IN THE MEETING SITUATION

Rule 34 states that a vessel, "upon hearing the one or two blast signal of the other shall, if in agreement, sound the same whistle signal and take the steps necessary to effect a safe passing." In other words, the vessels should not turn unless agreement has been reached by whistle signals. The courts have ruled that in a meeting situation, course should not be altered until the approaching vessel answers with the same signal (one or two short blasts) unless to avoid immediate danger.[1]

Rule 34 further states that "if, however, from any cause, the vessel doubts the safety of the proposed maneuver, she shall sound the danger signal. . . ." The courts have also required the danger signal to be sounded if there are "cross signals"—one whistle answered with two, or two whistles answered with one. Rule 34 continues to say that after the danger signal is sounded, then "each vessel shall take appropriate precautionary action until a safe passing agreement is made." The precautionary action required by the courts has been

1. *Moore-McCormack Lines, Inc.* v. *S.S. Portmar*, D.C.N.Y. 1966, 249 F. Supp. 464 [head-on]. *In re Pacific Far East Line, Inc.*, D.C.Cal. 1970, 314 F. Supp. 1339 [starboard-to-starboard meeting].

to stop engines, and reverse if the proximity of the vessels requires it.[2] A vessel which answers two short blasts with the danger signal, and then sounds one short blast without stopping or reversing, is guilty of cross signals—even if the original proposal was an improper one. After stopping, signals must be exchanged before the vessels pass each other.

If a vessel does not answer your proposal, the best procedure is not to repeat the signal, but follow the same procedure outlined above—sound the danger signal and stop, until signals for passing with safety have been exchanged and understood.

BACKING SIGNAL

In a meeting situation, with the vessels in visual sight, any time either vessel puts her engines astern at any speed, she must sound three short blasts.

MEETING IN RESTRICTED WATERS

Rule 9, Narrow Channels, requires: "A vessel proceeding along the course of a narrow channel or fairway shall keep as near to the outer limit of the channel or fairway which lies on her starboard side as is safe and practicable." Therefore, if vessels are keeping to the right, passage should normally be port to port for vessels meeting in restricted waters. The courts have also held that:

In determining how vessels are approaching each other, in narrow tortuous channels like the one here in question, the general course in the channel must alone be considered, and not the course they may be on by the compass at any particular time while pursuing the windings and turnings of the channel.[3]

2. The *Fulton*, C.C.A.N.Y. 1931, 54 F. 2d 467.
3. The *Milwaukee*, 1871, Fed. Cas. No. 9, 626.

COLREGS SIGNALS FOR MEETING

In the COLREGS, both vessels are required to sound the appropriate maneuvering signals while they remain in sight of each other: one short blast when turning right, two short blasts when turning left, or three short blasts if backing down (although alteration of course is normally the most effective action in a meeting situation).

If vessels can pass safely port to port with no course change and without backing down, no signals are sounded.

The COLREGS make no mention of a starboard to starboard passage, which implies that such a passage is only proper when there is no risk of collision.

SUMMARY OF MEETING SIGNALS

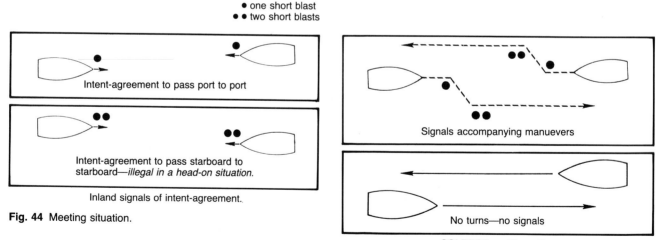

● one short blast
● ● two short blasts

Intent-agreement to pass port to port

Intent-agreement to pass starboard to starboard—*illegal in a head-on situation.*

Inland signals of intent-agreement.

Fig. 44 Meeting situation.

Signals accompanying manuevers

No turns—no signals

COLREGS: rudder-action signals only

7 Crossing Situation for Power-Driven Vessels

CROSSING SITUATION DEFINED

The definition of a crossing situation is the same in COLREGS Rule 15 and Inland Rule 15(a):

Rule 15—Crossing Situation

(a) When two power-driven vessels are crossing so as to involve risk of collision, the vessel which has the other on her starboard side shall keep out of the way and shall, if the circumstances of the case admit, avoid crossing ahead of the other vessel.

The crossing situation is best defined by what it is *not*. A crossing situation is an approach situation between two power-driven vessels in visual sight, but it is neither an overtaking nor a meeting situation.

Most students of the rules feel more comfortable with a definition that includes the relative bearing of the approaching vessel. Such a definition must satisfy all of the following requirements:

1. Vessel A holds vessel B in the arc between dead ahead and 22.5 degrees abaft the starboard beam.

2. Vessel B holds vessel A in the arc between dead ahead and 22.5 degrees abaft the port beam.

3. The vessels are not in a meeting situation.

In Figure 45, vessel A holds vessel B to starboard, so vessel A is the give-way vessel and is required to keep out of the way. Vessel B is the stand-on vessel and is required to maintain course and speed.

If only one sidelight is sighted at night, its meaning is similar to traffic lights: a green light means you are the stand-on vessel and you keep going; a red light means you must give way. In the first case, where a green light is initially sighted, if the give-way vessel turns right you will briefly observe both sidelights and then only the red sidelight.

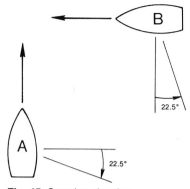

Fig. 45 Crossing situation.

The rules also specify what to do in a doubtful, borderline case. In Figure 47, if vessel B is in any doubt as to whether she is overtaking or crossing, she should assume that she is overtaking and keep out of the way.

In Figure 48, if vessel B is in any doubt as to whether she is crossing or meeting, she should assume that she is meeting and alter course to starboard for a port-to-port passing.

The stand-on vessel in a crossing situation is required to maintain course and speed. The stand-

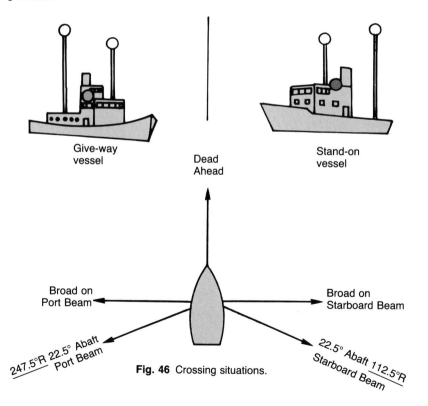

Fig. 46 Crossing situations.

on vessel can depart from the requirement to maintain course and speed under the following circumstances laid down in Rule 17, COLREGS and Inland Rules:

1. The stand-on vessel *may* take action to avoid collision by her maneuver alone, as soon as it becomes apparent to her that the give-way vessel is not taking appropriate action in compliance with these rules. The stand-on vessel shall, if the circumstances of the case admit, not alter course to port for a vessel on her own port side.
2. When, from any cause, the stand-on vessel finds herself so close that collision cannot be avoided by the action of the give-way vessel alone (i.e., she is in extremis), she *shall* take such action as will best help to avoid collision.

As mentioned before, the give-way vessel must keep out of the way. The other requirements of the give-way vessel must be emphasized. She must "take early and substantial action to keep well clear" and *avoid crossing ahead of the other vessel*.

The psychology of the crossing situation must be kept in mind by the give-way vessel when she plans her maneuver. The requirement placed on the stand-on vessel to maintain course and speed while the other vessel maneuvers to avoid collision can cause some anxious moments on the bridge. If the give-way vessel slows down to allow the stand-on vessel to cross ahead, such action may not be as readily apparent as turning smartly to starboard. A good guideline is always to turn to starboard so as to point astern of the stand-on vessel.

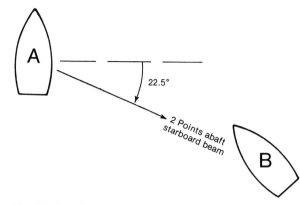

Fig. 47 Crossing or overtaking situation?

Fig. 48 Crossing or meeting situation?

INLAND SIGNALS FOR CROSSING

The whistle signals in the Inland Rules are signals of intent-agreement; the light signals are optional. The give-way vessel should normally keep out of the way by slowing or stopping her engines and/or turning right. In this case she would sound one short blast meaning "I intend to leave you on my port side." The stand-on vessel would then answer in agreement with one short blast. If the give-way vessel elects to reverse her engines in order to stop and let the stand-on vessel pass ahead, she would sound three short blasts.

Rule 34 also mentions an exchange of two short blasts—meaning "I intend to leave you on my starboard side"—but when are they "authorized or required by these Rules"? The only place in the rules where a vessel which has the other on her starboard side is specifically authorized to leave the other vessel to starboard in the crossing situation is in Rule 15(b). The provision here pertains to a vessel on the Great Lakes or Western Rivers (or waters specified by the Secretary). The vessel proceeding up or down the river has the right of way over a vessel crossing the river, regardless of whether the crossing vessel is to port or starboard.

Technically, there is nothing in the rules to prevent the give-way vessel from turning left, *providing* that she does not cross ahead of the other vessel. (In the past, there was a Pilot Rule which made a left turn illegal in the crossing situation.) In practice then, two short blasts has been a "road hog" signal used by a give-way vessel determined to ignore the rules and cross ahead of the stand-on vessel. For that reason, this writer recommends that you do not initiate a two blast signal in the crossing situation (except where provided on the Great Lakes or Western Rivers). The important question, then, is what to do if you are the stand-on vessel and the give-way vessel sounds two short blasts. This writer recommends that the two blast signal be immediately answered with the danger signal. Rule 34 states: "If, however, from any cause, the vessel doubts the safety of the proposed maneuver, she shall sound the danger signal . . . and each vessel shall take appropriate precautionary action until a safe passing agreement is made." Appropriate precautionary action according to past court rulings is stop engines, and reverse if the proximity of the vessels requires it.

The courts recognized long ago that "cross signals" in a crossing situation are a positive indication of a dangerous situation. If you sound one short blast and the other vessel crosses your signal (answers with two short blasts), you should sound the danger signal and stop—and reverse if the proximity of the vessels requires it.

COLREGS SIGNALS FOR CROSSING

In a crossing situation, the COLREGS state that the vessel which has the other on her own starboard side is the give-way vessel and is required to sound the appropriate one, two, or three short blasts as she maneuvers to keep out of the way.

A give-way vessel that takes avoiding action by turning left should not cross the projected course of the stand-on vessel. If a give-way vessel can keep out of the way by slowing or stopping her engines, she sounds no signals.

Normally the stand-on vessel will sound no signals unless it becomes necessary to sound the danger signal. If the stand-on vessel finds it necessary to maneuver as provided in Rule 17, she must accompany all maneuvers, including a maneuver in extremis, with the appropriate one, two, or three short blasts.

SUMMARY OF CROSSING SIGNALS

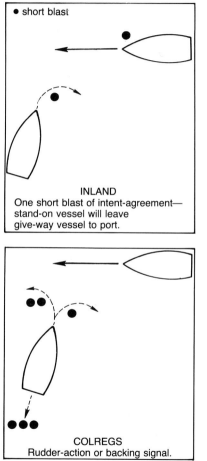

● short blast

INLAND
One short blast of intent-agreement—
stand-on vessel will leave
give-way vessel to port.

COLREGS
Rudder-action or backing signal.

Fig. 49 Crossing situation.

8 Law in Fog and Restricted Visibility

Except for the minor differences noted in this chapter, the rules in fog are the same in the COLREGS and in the Inland Rules. The rules that govern a vessel "navigating in or near an area of restricted visibility" are concerned with the following general types of requirements:

1. Proceeding at a "safe speed adapted to the prevailing circumstances and conditions of restricted visibility."
2. Obtaining early warning of risk of collision by maintaining a proper lookout by sight, hearing, radar, and any other available means.
3. Avoiding action when an approaching vessel is detected only on radar.
4. Avoiding action when a fog signal is heard from a vessel that has not been visually sighted.
5. Sounding the prescribed fog signals.

SAFE SPEED

Rule 6—Safe Speed

Every vessel shall at all times proceed at a safe speed so that she can take proper and effective action to avoid collision and be stopped within a distance appropriate to the prevailing circumstances and conditions.

In determining a safe speed the following factors shall be among those taken into account:

(a) By all vessels:
  (i) the state of visibility;
  (ii) the traffic density including concentration of fishing vessels or any other vessels;
  (iii) the maneuverability of the vessel with special reference to stopping distance and turning ability in the prevailing conditions;
  (iv) at night the presence of background light such as from shores lights or from back scatter of her own lights;

(v) the state of wind, sea, and current, and the proximity of navigational hazards;

(vi) the draft in relation to the available depth of water.

(b) Additionally, by vessels with operational radar:

(i) the characteristics, efficiency and limitations of the radar equipment;

(ii) any constraints imposed by the radar range scale in use;

(iii) the effect on radar detection of the sea state, weather, and other sources of interference;

(iv) the possibility that small vessels, ice and other floating objects may not be detected by radar at an adequate range;

(v) the number, location, and movement of vessels detected by radar; and

(vi) the more exact assessment of the visibility that may be possible when radar is used to determine the range of vessels or other objects in the vicinity.

Rule 19, Conduct of Vessels in Restricted Visibility, requires vessels to proceed at a "safe speed." Two of the factors which must be taken into account to determine a safe speed (Rule 6) are the state of visibility and the maneuverability of the vessel with special reference to stopping distance. In the writer's opinion, the "half distance rule" applied by the courts in the past will continue to be of major importance. The half distance rule requires a vessel to proceed at a speed which allows her to stop in a distance equal to half the prevailing visibility.

U.S. military vessels exceeding a safe speed due to operational commitments will be found at fault by the courts if the excessive speed contributes to a collision. The owners, the taxpayers of the United States, must pay the damages.

EARLY WARNING OF RISK OF COLLISION

Rule 5—Lookout

Every vessel shall at all times maintain a proper look-out by sight and hearing as well as by all available means appropriate in the prevailing circumstances and conditions so as to make a full appraisal of the situation and of the risk of collision.

Rule 7—Risk of Collision

(a) Every vessel shall use all available means appropriate to the prevailing circumstances and conditions to determine if risk of collision exists. If there is any doubt such risk shall be deemed to exist.

(b) Proper use shall be made of radar equipment if fitted and operational, including long-range scanning to obtain early warning of risk of collision and radar plotting or equivalent systematic observation of detected objects.

(c) Assumptions shall not be made on the basis of scanty information, especially scanty radar information.

(d) In determining if risk of collision exists the following considerations shall be among those taken into account:

(i) such risk shall be deemed to exist if the compass bearing of an approaching vessel does not appreciably change; and

(ii) such risk may sometimes exist even when an appreciable bearing change is evident, particularly when approaching a very large vessel or a tow or when approaching a vessel at close range.

Rules 5 and 7 make two facts very obvious: radar is not a substitute for a "proper lookout by sight and hearing," nor is a quick look at the radar enough. Rule 7 requires a radar plot or "equivalent systematic observation." A radar plot includes plotting directly on the scope or on a radar deflection plotter fitted over the scope. "Systematic observation" includes the plotting teams used on most naval vessels as well as computerized collision-avoidance systems which process radar bearing and range data and display information on a cathode-ray tube.

ACTIONS TO AVOID RADAR CONTACTS

Rule 19—Conduct of Vessels in Restricted Visibility

(d) A vessel which detects by radar alone the presence of another vessel shall determine if a close-quarters situation is developing or risk of collision exists. If so, she shall take avoiding action in ample time, provided that when such action consists of an alteration of course, so far as possible the following shall be avoided:

(i) an alteration of course to port for a vessel forward of the beam, other than for a vessel being overtaken; and

(ii) an alteration of course toward a vessel abeam or abaft the beam.

The requirements of Rule 8 also apply to actions taken in fog and restricted visibility:

Rule 8—Action to Avoid Collision

(a) Any action taken to avoid collision shall, if the circumstances of the case admit, be positive, made in ample time and with due regard to the observance of good seamanship.

(b) Any alteration of course or speed to avoid collision shall, if the circumstances of the case admit, be large enough to be readily apparent to another vessel observing visually or by radar; a succession of small alterations of course or speed should be avoided.

(c) If there is sufficient sea room, alteration of course alone may be the most effective action to avoid a close-quarters situation provided that it is made in good time, is substantial and does not result in another close-quarters situation.

(d) Action taken to avoid collision with another vessel shall be such as to result in passing at a safe distance. The effectiveness of the action shall be carefully checked until the other vessel is finally past and clear.

(e) If necessary to avoid collision or allow more time to assess the situation, a vessel shall slacken her speed or take all way off by stopping or reversing her means of propulsion.

ACTIONS WHEN A FOG SIGNAL IS HEARD (Rule 19(e))

Except where it has been determined that a risk of collision does not exist, every vessel which hears apparently forward of her beam the fog signal of another vessel, or which cannot avoid a close-quarters situation with another vessel forward of her beam, shall reduce her speed to the minimum at which she can be kept on course. She shall if necessary take all her way off and, in any event, navigate with extreme caution until danger of collision is over.

This rule requires that a vessel slow down to bare steerageway whenever a fog signal is heard apparently forward of the beam, "except where it has been determined that a risk of collision does not exist." We must assume that the rule refers to the use of radar to make the determination that risk of collision does not exist. A cautionary note is appropriate here, as the process of matching radar contacts with fog signals heard is subject to error. One reason is that sound is deceptive in fog—it is very difficult to determine the direction from which a fog signal is coming. The other factor is contained in Rule 6: "the possibility that small vessels . . . may not be detected by radar at an adequate range." Under ordinary conditions, this should not be a factor with a radar of recent design. It can, however, become an important factor when the radar is in a degraded state, or in conditions of restricted visibility caused by thunderstorms which give a radar return. The possibility exists that a maneuver to avoid a radar contact may result in a turn toward the vessel whose signal was heard (Figure 50).

COURT RULINGS ON RADAR

The courts have made a number of rulings on radar-equipped vessels:

Only contact on radar

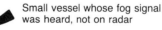
Small vessel whose fog signal was heard, not on radar

Fig. 50 Matching radar contacts with fog signals.

1. Radar is not an excuse for exceeding safe speed.[1]
2. Dependable radar equipment must be turned on and intelligent and reasonable use made of it.[2]
3. A vessel rigging her booms in such a way as to greatly impair effective use of her radar is guilty of gross negligence.[3]
4. A fog bank must be searched with radar, and the vessel shall reduce speed or stop if necessary until it has been done.[4]
5. The greater the speed at which a vessel is traveling, the greater should be the range setting of her radar.[5]
6. The radar bearing of an approaching vessel which remains fairly constant is indicative of a collision course and requires immediate and radical avoiding action by the observing vessel.[6]

A district court required the following actions of a radar-equipped vessel:

> When the Norscot sighted the Harrison on radar, two miles distant, bearing dead ahead, and the Norscot was proceeding at a speed of 14 knots, she was already in an emergency situation and her engines should have been immediately backed full, her helm put hard right, and her anchors dropped.[7]

1. *Norscot Shipping Co.* v. *S.S. President Harrison,* D.C.Pa. 1970, 308 F. Supp. 1100.
2. *U.S.* v. *M/V Wuerttemberg,* D.C.S.C. 1963, 219 F. Supp. 211.
3. *Hess Shipping Corp.* v. *S.S. Charles Lykes,* D.C.Ala. 1968, 285 F. Supp. 412.
4. *U.S.* v. *M/V Wuerttemberg, supra.*
5. *Norscot Shipping Co.* v. *S.S. President Harrison, supra.*
6. *Ibid.*
7. *Ibid.*

FOG SIGNALS

The rules contain no recommendation as to what distance should be used to determine if visibility is restricted for the purpose of sounding fog signals. Textbook-writers have long recommended the required visibility of sidelights as a guideline, which is now *three miles* for vessels of 50 meters or more in length.

All the prescribed fog signals for vessels underway are given on the whistle at intervals of not more than two minutes. The signals prescribed for a vessel at anchor or aground are given on a bell, or on a bell and gong, at intervals of not more than one minute. The optional whistle signals for a pilot vessel, a vessel at anchor, and a vessel aground may be sounded as required but *in addition to* the prescribed signals. The short-prolonged-short signal may be used by a vessel at anchor to give warning of her position and of the possibility of collision to an approaching vessel.

In the Inland Rules only, the following vessels are not required to sound the fog signals for a vessel at anchor when in designated special anchorage areas: "a vessel of less than 20 meters in length; and a barge, canal boat, scow, or other nondescript craft" (Inland Rule 35(j)).

FOG SIGNALS[8]

KEY: — prolonged blast, 4–6 seconds
     · short blast, about one second
     S distinct stroke on bell
  BELL rapid ringing of bell for 5 seconds forward
 GONG rapid sounding of gong for 5 seconds aft

VESSELS UNDERWAY

CATEGORY	SIGNAL
	given at intervals of not more than two minutes
Power-driven vessel making way through the water	—
Power-driven vessel, underway but stopped and making no way through the water	— —
Vessel not under command	
Vessel restricted in her ability to maneuver	
Sailing vessel	— · ·
Vessel engaged in fishing	
Vessel engaged in towing or pushing	
COLREGS *only*: Vessel constrained by her draft	— · ·
Vessel towed	— · · ·

VESSELS NOT UNDERWAY

CATEGORY	SIGNAL	INTERVAL
Vessel at anchor:		
length less than 100 meters	BELL	1 minute
length 100 meters or greater	BELL/GONG	1 minute
Any vessel at anchor may, also, sound	· — ·	As required
Vessel aground:		
length less than 100 meters	SSS/BELL/SSS	1 minute
length 100 meters or greater	SSS/BELL/SSS/GONG	1 minute
Any vessel aground may, also, sound	APPROPRIATE WHISTLE SIGNAL*	As required
Vessel restricted in her ability to maneuver, at anchor	— · ·	2 minutes
Vessel engaged in fishing, at anchor	— · ·	2 minutes

*See meanings of "F", "U", and "V" in Appendix B.
Note: Vessels moored at the end of a pier have been required by the courts to "make some noise with a horn, a bell, a gong, or the like."[9]

8. (1) Pilot vessel may in addition sound 4 short blasts, as required, as an identity signal.
   (2) A vessel of less than 12 meters in length shall not be obliged to give the following signals but, if she does not, shall make some other efficient sound signal at intervals of not more than 2 minutes.

9. The *Youngstown*, C.C.A.N.Y. 1930, 40 F. 2d 420.

9 Special Circumstances

In Rule 2 (COLREGS and Inland Rules) the expression *special circumstances* is used in two ways. Paragraph (a) recognizes that special circumstances may require precautions or actions *in addition to* the specific requirements of the other rules. (Chapter 10 deals with this subject.) Paragraph (b) of the same rule, quoted below, states that special circumstances may require a *departure* from the other rules in order to avoid "immediate danger."

> (b) In construing and complying with these Rules due regard shall be had to all dangers of navigation and collision and to any special circumstances, including the limitations of the vessels involved, which may make a departure from these Rules necessary to avoid immediate danger.

Special circumstances refers primarily to situations which have not been provided for in the rules. It is possible, however, to consider an example where departure from a requirement of the rules is specifically provided for in the rules themselves. The stand-on vessel in a crossing situation is required by Rule 17(a)(i) to maintain course and speed. The rule goes on to describe when a vessel *may* depart from that requirement, and then describes the circumstance under which she *shall* depart from that requirement:

Rule 17—Action by Stand-on Vessel

> (ii) The latter vessel may, however, take action to avoid collision by her maneuver alone, as soon as it becomes apparent to her that the vessel required to keep out of the way is not taking appropriate action in compliance with these rules.
>
> (b) When, from any cause, the vessel required to keep her course and speed finds herself so close that collision cannot be avoided by the action of the give-way vessel alone, she shall take such action as will best aid to avoid collision.

Paragraph (b) of Rule 17 is an example of where action is required in extremis. Vessels are in extremis whenever they are in such close proximity, regardless of the cause, that adherence to the ordinary rules is certain to cause a collision. The rules do not tell a vessel in extremis to back down, or to turn left or right; vessels must "take such action as will best aid to avoid collision."

When it becomes apparent that a collision will occur, vessels must be maneuvered in such a way as to minimize damage and loss of life. The primary concern in a collision is to avoid striking at such an angle that the bow of one vessel cuts into the side of the other.

In special circumstances, *both* vessels are give-way vessels and both are required to take action to avoid collision. Special circumstances—other than in extremis—have been deemed to exist in the following types of situations:

Vessel unable to comply with the rules
Approach of a third vessel
Situations not covered by the rules
Departure from the rules by agreement
(Primarily Inland Rules)

VESSEL UNABLE TO COMPLY WITH THE RULES

It is possible for a vessel to get into a situation where it is not physically possible for her to carry out her obligations under the rules. An example is a tug with tow astern (Figure 51): if she stopped suddenly to avoid a crossing vessel, her own tow would collide with her stern. In such a situation, the tug should sound the danger signal to warn the other vessel of her inability to comply with the rules.

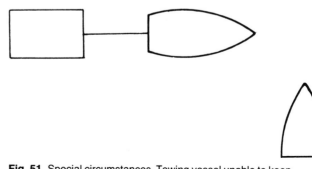

Fig. 51 Special circumstances. Towing vessel unable to keep out of the way.

It is possible under the Inland Rules that the tug may choose to sound two short blasts rather than the danger signal. The stand-on vessel would be justified, due to the special circumstances, in answering the two short blasts with the same signal, and maneuvering to keep out of the way of the tug. Regardless of the signals chosen, the stand-on vessel must recognize the apparent conditions and give way. She cannot insist on the right of way in the face of special circumstances.

A towing vessel is, however, not automatically given the right of way. If a crossing vessel can be avoided by slowing down in a timely manner, special circumstances do not exist.

APPROACH OF A THIRD VESSEL

As previously stated, *special circumstances* refers primarily to situations which have not been provided for in the rules. One possibility is the case where three or more vessels are approaching simultaneously. A vessel in such circumstances may find herself the stand-on vessel with respect to one vessel, and the give-way vessel with respect to another. She would therefore be required to maneuver with respect to one and to maintain course and speed with respect to the other—a physical impossibility.

In some cases, more than two vessels may approach each other simultaneously in such a way that signals and maneuvers cannot be handled one at a time. Figure 52 illustrates a case where a schooner was towed out from a pier and ran across a channel between meeting vessels.

In a normal situation both vessels would be required to alter course to starboard when meeting head-on. Here, both vessels turned to cross under

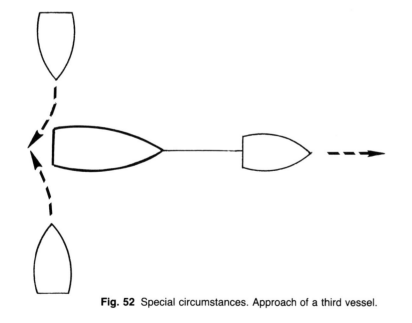

Fig. 52 Special circumstances. Approach of a third vessel.

the stern of the schooner and collided. Both vessels were found at fault for failure to recognize the special circumstances and stop.[1] Bridge-to-bridge communications would obviously be of great assistance in situations that involve three or more vessels.

SITUATIONS NOT COVERED BY THE RULES

There are some situations for which the rules provide no specific guidance as to how to maneuver with respect to the other vessel. Examples include approach situations where one or both vessels are entering or leaving a slip, maneuvering around piers, or backing. In each case at least one vessel is not on a steady course, and the rules provide no directions on how to maneuver if an approaching vessel cannot be avoided without one of them taking action. Such situations are "special circumstances" and the rules for meeting, crossing, or overtaking do not apply.

A typical example of how actions in special circumstances would differ from actions required by the other rules would be the case where a vessel on a steady course sights a vessel on her port hand crossing her course while maneuvering around piers. In Figure 53, vessel A would be the stand-on vessel under the rules for the crossing situation, while the proper action in special circumstances might be to maneuver to the right in order to give the other vessel a wider berth.

The courts have ruled that a vessel moving from her dock or berth is in "special circumstances" until settled on her course. Even in special cir-

1. *Shaw* v. *The Reading and the David Smith*, D.C. Pa. 1888, 38 F. 269.

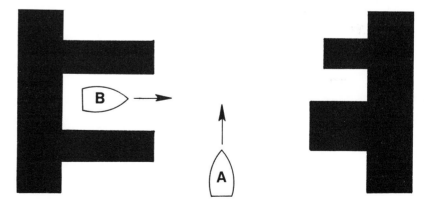

Fig. 53 Special circumstances. Vessel B maneuvering around piers.

cumstances, a backing vessel may signal her desire to cross ahead of an approaching vessel. The crossing rules do not apply, but by treating the stern of the backing vessel as the bow for the purpose of signals, she can make her desires known by one or two short blasts, depending on whether the approaching vessel is to the port or starboard of her "bow" (Figure 54, A and B). Such a signal is a proposal only; neither vessel is permitted or required by the rules to maintain course and speed.

A vessel which is backing in such a way that she is not crossing the course of another vessel is in a slightly different situation. She may be in a position where she is obstructing a channel or fairway while in the process of twisting toward her intended course. A vessel approaching from more than 22.5° abaft her beam has been considered an overtaking vessel, even in cases where the twisting vessel was stopped in the water or making some sternway.

Figure 54 shows that a signal of two short blasts results in the approaching vessel leaving the backing vessel on her own starboard hand whether the backing vessel is crossing her course (situation A) or being overtaken (situation C). One short blast results in the backing vessel being left on the port hand in situations B and D.

The most common cause of collision involving a vessel leaving her slip with the proper signals is another vessel passing too near to pier ends at too great a speed.

Rule 2, Responsibility, has also modified the requirement for the stand-on vessel. The stand-on vessel is legally maintaining course and speed when maneuvering in the following ways:

1. Stopping her engine and checking her speed preparatory to her landing.[2]
2. Following a channel course that of necessity curves around bends.[3]
3. Stopping to pick up a pilot.[4]

The stand-on vessel is required to maneuver in extremis and may maneuver making "such necessary variations in her course as will enable her to avoid immediate danger arising from natural obstructions to navigation."[5]

DEPARTURE FROM THE RULES BY AGREEMENT (PRIMARILY INLAND RULES)

Departure from the Rules by agreement pertains primarily to the Inland Rules because Inland whistle signals are signals of intent-agreement. The one- and two-short-blast signals in the COLREGS are not—they are rudder-action signals; agreement to depart from the rules could conceivably be reached through radio communications, however.

One situation where departure by agreement can occur is the meeting situation in Inland waters where the vessels are meeting head-on. Vessels who agree to pass starboard to starboard in a head-on situation (which is illegal), by the exchange of two-blast signals, place themselves in special circumstances. If a collision results, the vessel proposing the departure is certain to be found at fault unless the proposal was necessitated by immediate

2. The *D.S.* No. 24, D.C.N.Y. 1943, 52 F. Supp. 648.
3. The *Interstate*, D.C.N.Y. 1922, 280 F. 446.
4. *U.S.* v. *S.S. Soya Atlantic*, C.A. Md. 1964, 330 F. 2d 732.
5. The *John L. Hasbrouck*, 23 L. Ed. 962.

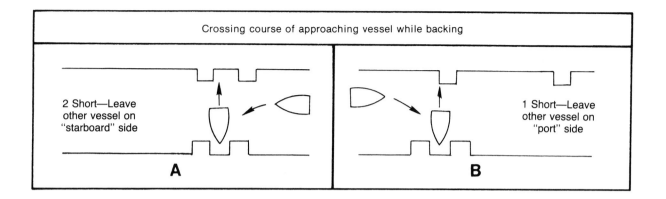

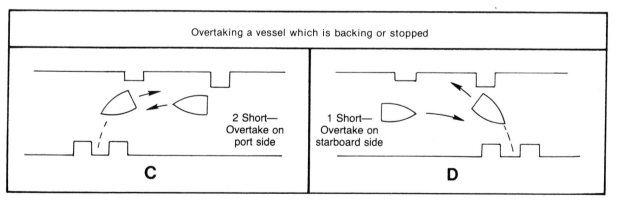

Fig. 54 Special circumstances involving a backing vessel.

danger. The proposal is not binding on the other vessel, and she may therefore be found at fault for the agreement.

A two-short-blast signal in the Inland Rules means "I intend to leave you on my starboard side." As mentioned in the chapter on the crossing situation, the important question on the bridge of the stand-on vessel is: does the two-blast signal from the other vessel mean "I intend to *cross your bow* and leave you on my starboard side," *or* "I intend to leave you on my starboard side without crossing your projected path"? The first case involves crossing the bow of the stand-on vessel, which is a departure from the rules; the second case does not violate any of the rules. Since the Inland Rules do not answer the question just posed, it is the writer's opinion that we should assume that two blasts in the crossing situation is a proposal to cross the bow of the stand-on vessel. Therefore, a stand-on vessel agreeing to the proposal by answering with two blasts places herself in special circumstances.

In any situation involving special circumstances, all the vessels involved must exercise extreme caution, and take whatever action is most likely to avoid collision.

10 Good Seamanship

Chapter 9 discussed special circumstances that may require a *departure* from the other rules. Circumstances may also require precautions *in addition to* those specified in the rules. The responsibility to take additional precautions as dictated by the special circumstances of a particular case, or by the ordinary practice of seamen, is placed on the mariner by Rule 2(a):

> Nothing in these Rules shall exonerate any vessel, or the owner, master, or crew thereof, from the consequences of any neglect to comply with these Rules or of the neglect of any precaution which may be required by the ordinary practice of seamen, or by the special circumstances of the case.

Many of the requirements of "good seamanship" have been included in the latest revision of the rules. Note that Subpart I of the Steering and Sailing Rules concerns "Conduct of Vessels in *Any* Condition of Visibility." Thus, the factors discussed in Chapter 8 for determining a safe speed in fog also must be taken into consideration in determining a safe speed in clear weather. The requirements in Rule 8, Action to Avoid Collision, are also typical requirements of good seamanship—action taken to avoid collision should be easily understood by an observing vessel, as well as being the action which is most likely to avoid a collision.

Rules 9 and 10 sensibly advise all vessels to avoid anchoring in a narrow channel or traffic-separation scheme, or in areas near the termination of a traffic-separation scheme.

The requirements discussed in Chapter 8, concerning the maintenance of a proper lookout by sight, hearing, radar, and any other available means, are applicable in clear weather as well as in conditions of restricted visibility. Note how Rules 5 and 7 (pp. 57–58) complement each other, which is as it should be, since maintaining a proper lookout is an integral part of determining if a risk of collision exists.

Generally, any condition that causes a deviation from the norm may require additional precautions. Consider the following factors which may cause additional precautions to be taken:

1. Adverse weather conditions.
2. Unusual conditions of loading or trim.
3. Failure or degradation of any equipment important to safe navigation.
4. Traffic density.
5. Proximity of navigational hazards.
6. Availability of external aids to navigation.
7. Transport of dangerous cargo or cargo that poses a threat to the environment.

Apart from provisions of good seamanship in the rules, the following list gives specific requirements that the courts have found reasonable. Many items listed might lead us to believe that Rule 2(a) is politely telling us to use common sense in navigating our vessel.

1. Speed in good visibility
   a. must comply with local regulations,
   b. must not create swell or suction which would cause damage to other vessels, and
   c. must be such that our vessel is completely under control.
2. Vessels must not pass unnecessarily near to pier ends.
3. Vessels must be properly manned and steered.
4. Vessels must not navigate with defective equipment.

5. A vessel has the "responsibility to utilize available weather reports so that it can operate in manner consistent with foreseeable risk."[1]
6. Vessels moored must have sufficient mooring lines.
7. Anchored vessels must have sufficient chain out, and drop a second anchor if the circumstances require it.
8. "A navigator is chargeable with knowledge of the maneuvering capacity of his vessel. He is bound to know the character of his vessel and how she would turn in ordinary conditions."[2]
9. "When a vessel is known to be about to enter or leave a dock, other vessels should keep well clear and avoid embarrassing her maneuvers."[3]
10. "In waters well frequented by small tows . . . the law requires that a ship should have a competent person standing by in the forecastle ready at a moment's notice to let go the anchors."[4]
11. "Where two steamers about to meet are running one with and the other against the tide, if it be necessary that one or the other should stop in order to avoid a collision, the one proceeding against the tide should stop."[5]

1. *M. P. Howlett Inc.* v. *Tug Dalzellido*, D.C.N.Y. 1971, 324 F. Supp. 912.
2. *City of New York* v. *Morania No. 12 Inc.*, 1973, 357 F. Supp. 234.
3. *Ibid.*
4. *River Terminals Corp.* v. *U.S.*, D.C. La. 1954, 121 F. Supp. 98.
5. The *Galatea*, N.Y. 1876, 23 L. Ed. 727.

12. Special circumstances may require that an anchor watch be maintained.
13. Vessels must not anchor too close to other vessels already at anchor.

The courts have also given legal meaning to the term *proper lookout.*

1. "Lookout is person who is specially charged with duty of observing lights, sounds, echoes, or any obstruction to navigation."[6]
2. "Lookouts, who must be kept on all vessels, must be persons of suitable experience, properly stationed on vessel, and actually and vigilantly employed in the performance of that duty."[7]
3. "Lookout should be placed as low and as far as possible."[8] This is a requirement in clear weather as well as in fog if failure to comply can result in any one of the following:
   a. the lookout does not have a clear, unobstructed view,
   b. the lookout's ability to hear signals is impaired, and
   c. the lookout will sight a danger earlier if placed forward (as when leaving a blind slip).
4. "Lookout . . . should have no other duties."[9]
5. The circumstances will dictate the number of lookouts required. The number must be sufficient to detect any reasonably foreseen danger from any direction.
6. A lookout astern is required when backing.

6. *Sun Oil Co.* v. *S.S. Georgel*, D.C.N.Y. 1969, 245 F. Supp. 537.
7. *Jett* v. *Texas Co.*, D.C. Del. 1947, 73 F. Supp. 699.
8. The *Kaga Maru*, D.C. Wash. 1927, 18 F. 2d 295.

7. Lookouts must have a direct and positive means of communicating what they observe to the conning officer. "If the lookout cannot, or does not, report his observations, improper watch is being maintained."[10] A lookout cannot wear headphones, as his ability to hear signals would be impaired.

NAVIGATION SAFETY REGULATIONS

The Coast Guard, acting under authority of the "Ports and Waterways Safety Act of 1972," issued Federal Regulations entitled "Navigation Safety Regulations." The regulations were issued on January 31, 1977, and apply to self-propelled vessels of 1,600 gross tons or more when operating on the navigable waters of the United States. Their general purpose is to set a minimum level of navigation practice and equipment so as to reduce the risk of vessel casualties resulting from unprofessional performance or substandard equipment. They are included in this chapter because many of their requirements are requirements of "good seamanship."

164.01 Applicability.
This part applies to each self-propelled vessel of 1600 or more gross tons when it is operating in or on the navigable waters of the United States, except the Panama Canal and the St. Lawrence Seaway.

164.11 Navigation underway: general.
The owner, master, or person in charge of each vessel underway shall ensure that:

9. *U.S.* v. The *Holland*, D.C. Md. 1957, 151 F. Supp. 772.
10. *U.S.* v. *Tug Collette Malloy*, C.C.A. Tex. 1975, 507 F. 2d 1019.

(a) the wheelhouse is constantly manned by persons who—
  (1) Direct and control the movement of the vessel; and
  (2) Fix the vessel's position;
(b) Each person performing a duty described in paragraph (a) of this section is competent to perform that duty;
(c) The position of the vessel at each fix is plotted on a chart of the area and the person directing the movement of the vessel is informed of the vessel's position.
(d) Electronic and other navigational equipment, external fixed aids to navigation, geographic reference points, and hydrographic contours are used when fixing the vessel's position;
(e) Buoys alone are not used to fix the vessel's position;

NOTE.—Buoys are aids to navigation placed in approximate positions to alert the mariner to hazards to navigation or to indicate the orientation of a channel. Buoys may not maintain an exact position because strong or varying currents, heavy seas, ice, and collisions with vessels can move or sink them or set them adrift. Although buoys may corroborate a position fixed by other means, buoys cannot be used to fix a position; however, if no other aids are available, buoys alone may be used to establish an estimated position.

(f) The danger of each closing visual or each closing radar contact is evaluated and the person directing the movement of the vessel knows the evaluation;
(g) Rudder orders are executed as given;
(h) Engine speed and direction orders are executed as given;

(i) Magnetic variation and deviation and gyrocompass errors are known and correctly applied by the person directing the movement of the vessel;
(j) A person whom he has determined is competent to steer the vessel is in the wheelhouse at all times[11];
(k) If a pilot other than a member of the vessel's crew is employed, the pilot is informed of the draft, maneuvering characteristics, and peculiarities of the vessel and of any abnormal circumstances on the vessel that may affect its safe navigation;
(l) Current velocity and direction for the area to be transited are known by the person directing the movement of the vessel;
(m) Predicted set and drift are known by the person directing the movement of the vessel;
(n) Tidal state for the area to be transited is known by the person directing movement of the vessel;
(o) The vessel's anchors are ready for letting go;
(p) The person directing the movement of the vessel sets the vessel's speed with consideration for—
  (1) The prevailing visibility and weather conditions;
  (2) The proximity of the vessel to fixed shore and marine structures;
  (3) The tendency of the vessel underway to squat and suffer impairment of maneuverability when there is small underkeel clearance;

11. See also 46 U.S.C. 672 which requires an able seaman at the wheel on U.S. vessels of 100 gross or more in narrow or crowded waters during low visibility.

(4) The comparative proportions of the vessel and the channel;

(5) The density of marine traffic;

(6) The damage that might be caused by the vessel's wake;

(7) The strength and direction of the current; and

(8) Any local vessel speed limit;

(q) The tests required by 164.25 are made and recorded in the vessel's log; and

(r) The equipment required by this part is maintained in operable condition.

164.15   Navigation underway: confined or congested waters.

In the confined or congested waters described in 164.16, the master or person in charge of each vessel underway shall ensure that—

(a) Propulsion machinery can respond immediately through its full operating range;

(b) The engine room, including the main control station even if it is not in the engine room, is manned to operate the propulsion machinery as required by paragraph (a) of this section;

(c) Persons are available to rapidly anchor the vessel in an emergency; and

(d) The automatic pilot is not in use.

164.16   List of confined or congested waters. [Reserved]

164.19   Requirements for vessels at anchor.

The master or person in charge of each vessel that is anchored shall ensure that—

(a) A proper anchor watch is maintained;

(b) Procedures are followed to detect a dragging anchor; and

(c) Whenever weather, tide, or current conditions are likely to cause the vessel's anchor to drag, action is taken to ensure the safety of the vessel, structures, and other vessels, such as being ready to veer chain, let go a second anchor, or get underway using the vessel's own propulsion or tug assistance.

164.25   Tests before entering or getting underway.

No person may cause a vessel to enter into or get underway on the navigable waters of the United States unless, no more than 12 hours before entering or getting underway, the following equipment has been tested:

(a) Primary and secondary steering gear.

(b) All internal vessel control communications and vessel control alarms.

(c) Standby or emergency generator for as long as necessary to show proper functioning, including steady state temperature and pressure readings.

(d) Storage batteries for emergency lighting and power systems in vessel control and propulsion machinery spaces.

(e) Main propulsion machinery, ahead and astern.

164.30   Charts, publications, and equipment: general.

No person may operate or cause the operation of a vessel unless the vessel has the charts, publications, and equipment as required by 164.33 through 164.41 of this part.

164.33   Charts and publications.

(a) Each vessel must have the following:

(1) Except as provided by paragraph (b) of this section, charts of the area to be

transited published by the National Ocean Survey, U.S. Army Corps of Engineers, or a river authority that—

 (i) are of a large enough scale and have enough detail to enable safe navigation of the area; and

 (ii) are the most recently published and available for the area and currently corrected.

(2) Except as provided by paragraph (b) of this section, the most recent, available, and currently corrected copy of, or applicable extract from, each of the following publications, if it includes the area to be transited:

 (i) U.S. Coast Pilot.

 (ii) Coast Guard Light List.

 (iii) Notices to Mariners published by Defense Mapping Agency Hydrographic Center and Local Coast Guard Notice to Mariners.

 (iv) Tide Tables published by the National Ocean Survey.

 (v) Tidal Current Tables published by the National Ocean Survey, or river current publication issued by the U.S. Army, Corps of Engineers, or a river authority.

(b) A vessel may have a chart or publication published by a foreign government instead of a chart or publication required by this section if the chart or publication contains similar information to the U.S. Government publication or chart. A vessel bound from a foreign port to a port in the United States may have the latest charts and publications that were available at previous ports of call.

164.35 Equipment: all vessels.

Each vessel must have the following:

(a) A marine radar system for surface navigation.

(b) An illuminated magnetic steering compass, mounted in a binnacle, that can be read at the vessel's main steering stand.

(c) A current magnetic compass deviation table or graph or compass comparison record for the steering compass, in the wheelhouse.

(d) A gyrocompass.

(e) An illuminated repeater for the gyrocompass required by paragraph (d) of this section that is at the main steering stand, unless that gyrocompass is illuminated and is at the main steering stand.

(f) An illuminated rudder angle indicator in the wheelhouse.

(g) The following maneuvering information prominently displayed on a fact sheet in the wheelhouse:

 (1) For full and half speed, a turning circle diagram to port and starboard that shows the time and distance of advance and transfer required to alter the course 90 degrees with maximum rudder angle and constant power settings.

 (2) The time and distance to stop the vessel from full and half speed while maintaining approximately the initial heading with minimum application of rudder.

 (3) For each vessel with a fixed propeller, a table of shaft revolutions per minute for a representative range of speeds.

 (4) For each vessel with a controllable

pitch propeller, a table of control settings for a representative range of speeds.

(5) For each vessel that is fitted with an auxiliary device to assist in maneuvering, such as a bow thruster, a table of vessel speeds at which the auxiliary device is effective in maneuvering the vessel.

(6) The maneuvering information for the normal load and normal ballast condition for—

(i) Calm weather—wind 10 knots or less, calm sea;

(ii) No current;

(iii) Deep water conditions—water depth twice the vessel's draft or greater; and

(iv) Clean hull.

(7) At the bottom of the fact sheet, the following statement:

Warning

The response of the (name of the vessel) may be different from that listed above if any of the following conditions, upon which the maneuvering information is based, are varied:

(1) Calm weather—wind 10 knots or less, calm sea;

(2) No current;

(3) Water depth twice the vessel's draft or greater;

(4) Clean hull; and

(5) Intermediate drafts or unusual trim.

(h) An echo depth sounding device.

(i) A device that can continuously record the depth readings of the vessel's echo depth sounding device.

(j) Equipment on the bridge for plotting relative motion.

164.37 Equipment: Vessels of 10,000 gross tons or more.

(a) Each vessel of 10,000 gross tons or more must have, in addition to the radar system under 164.35 (a), a second marine radar system that operates independently of the first.

NOTE.—Independent operation means two completely separate systems, from separate branch power supply circuits or distribution panels to antennas, so that failure of any component of one system will not render the other system inoperative.

(b) On each tanker of 10,000 gross tons or more that is subject to Section 5 of the Port and Tanker Safety Act of 1978 (46 U.S.C. 391a), the dual radar system required by this part must have a short range capability and a long range capability and each radar must have true north features consisting of a display that is stabilized in azimuth.

(Titles I and II, 86 Stat. 426, 427 (33 U.S.C. 1224; 46 U.S.C. 391a); 49 CFR 1.46(n)(4).)

164.41 Electronic Position Fixing Devices.

(a) This section applies to vessels calling at ports in the continental U.S., including Alaska south of Cape Prince of Wales, except those vessels owned or bareboat charted and operated by the United States, by a state or its political subdivision, or by a foreign nation, and not engaged in commerce.

(b) Each vessel must have one of the following devices installed:

(1) A Loran-C receiver meeting paragraph (c) of this section.

(2) A continual update, satellite-based hybrid receiver meeting paragraph (d) of this section.

(3) A system that is found by the Commandant to meet the intent of the statements of availability, coverage, and accuracy for the U.S. Coastal Confluence Zone (CCZ) contained in the U.S. "Department of Transportation (DOT) National Plan for Navigation" (Report No. DOT-TST-78-4, dated November 1977). A person desiring a finding by the Commandant under this subparagraph must submit a written request describing the device to: Commandant (G-WLE/73), U.S. Coast Guard, Washington, D.C. 20950. After reviewing the request, the Commandant may require additional information to establish whether or not the device meets the intent of the "DOT National Plan for Navigation."

NOTE.—The "DOT National Plan for Navigation" is available from the National Technical Information Service, Springfield, VA 22161. Government Accession No. AD-A 052269.

(c) Each Loran-C receiver installed after May 31, 1979 must meet the following:

(1) Be a Type I or II receiver as defined in Section 1.2(e), meeting Part 2 (Minimum Performance Standards) of the Radio Technical Commission for Marine Services (RTCM) Paper 12-78/DO-100 dated December 20, 1977, and entitled "Minimum Performance Standards (MPS) Marine Loran-C Receiving Equipment". The standards referred to in this subparagraph are intended to be incorporated by reference as they exist on December 20, 1977 and notice of any change in these standards will be published in the Federal Register. This incorporation by reference was approved by the Director of the Federal Register on May 25, 1979 and is available for inspection at the Office of the Federal Register Library, Room 8401, 1100 L St. NW, Washington, D.C. 20408. The RTMC paper is available from the Radio Technical Commission for Marine Services, P.O. Box 19087, Washington, D.C. 20038 ((202) 298-6610).

(2) After June 1, 1982, except as allowed by paragraph (c)(3) of this section, have a permanently affixed label containing—

(i) The name and address of the manufacturer, and

(ii) The following statement:
This receiver was designed and manufactured to comply with Part 2 (Minimum Performance Standards) of the RTCM MPS for Marine Loran-C Receiving Equipment.

(3) Each Loran-C receiver installed before June 1, 1982, that meets paragraph (c)(1) of this section must meet

paragraph (c)(2) of this section on June 1, 1985.

(d) Each hybrid satellite system must have—
  (1) Automatic acquisition of satellite signals after initial operator settings have been entered;
  (2) Position updates derived from satellite information obtained during each usable satellite pass; and
  (3) A continual tracking intergrated [*sic*] complementary system that provides automatically, in between satellite passes, position updates at intervals of one minute or less.

(e) Each satellite navigation receiver installed before June 1, 1982, that meets paragraphs (d)(1) and (2), of this section must meet paragraph (d)(3) of this section on June 1, 1985.

164.51 Deviations from rules: emergency.

Except for the requirements of 164.53 (b), in an emergency, any person may deviate from any rule in this part to the extent necessary to avoid endangering persons, property, or the environment.

164.53 Deviations from rules and reporting: non-operating equipment.

(a) If during a voyage any equipment required by this part stops operating properly, the person directing the movement of the vessel may complete the voyage subject to the requirements in Part 160 of this chapter.

(b) If the vessel's radar, radio navigation receivers, gyrocompass, echo depth sounding device, or primary steering gear stops operating properly, the person directing the movement of the vessel must report or cause to be reported that it is not operating properly to the nearest Captain of the Port or Coast Guard District Commander as soon as possible.

164.55 Deviations from rules: continuing operation or period of time.

The Captain of the Port, upon written application, may authorize a deviation from any rule in this part if he determines that the deviation does not impair the safe navigation of the vessel under anticipated conditions and will not result in a violation of the rules for preventing collisions at sea. The authorization may be issued for vessels operating in the waters under the jurisdiction of the Captain of the Port for any continuing operation or period of time the Captain of the Port specifies.

164.61 Marine casualty reporting and record retention.

When a vessel is involved in a marine casualty as defined in 46 CFR 4.03–1, the master or person in charge of the vessel shall—

(a) Ensure compliance with 46 CFR Subpart 4.05, "Notice of Marine Casualty and Voyage Records," and

(b) Ensure that the voyage records required by 46 CFR 4.05–15 are retained for—
  (1) 30 days after the casualty if the vessel remains in the navigable waters of the United States; or
  (2) 30 days after the return of the vessel to a United States port if the vessel departs the navigable waters of the United States within 30 days after the marine casualty.

Effective date: This rule becomes effective on June 1, 1977.

11 Approach Situations As Viewed On Radar

Radar can be used to determine risk of collision in any condition of visibility. Holding a radar contact whose range is decreasing while the bearing remains nearly constant gives the same warning of a collision course as does a constant visual bearing. However, a series of visual bearings must always be taken when conditions permit, whether or not radar plotting is in use. A minimum amount of plotting to produce CPA range and bearing is required if a grease pencil is used directly on the radar scope.

One simple procedure is periodically to mark the position of radar contacts with a grease pencil and label with time (equal time intervals are preferred but not required). The line formed by the marks can be projected past the center of the scope as shown in Figure 55 (the direction of the line is the direction of relative motion, or DRM).

CPA bearing and range can be obtained by lining up the cursor perpendicular to the contact's projected track.

In practice, radar contacts in restricted visibility are often avoided by using only the CPA information obtained from the procedures outlined above. In Figure 56, the line projected from the center of the scope represents a heading marker. A radar contact is being plotted which indicates that the vessels are on near-collision courses. With the information given, we do not readily know if the contact is headed toward us or away from us. In this example it makes little difference, as a *substantial* change of course to starboard is appropriate in either case. We must continue to watch the contact to ensure that our maneuver is having the desired effect, as illustrated in Figure 57.

In order to visualize different approach situations on radar, additional information must be considered. Take, for example, a radar contact dead ahead on a constant bearing with the range decreasing. The speed of our own vessel must be compared with the speed of relative motion (SRM) to determine if the contact is on the same

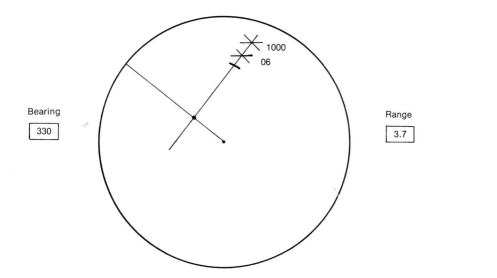

Bearing

330

Range

3.7

Fig. 55 Obtaining CPA bearing and range.

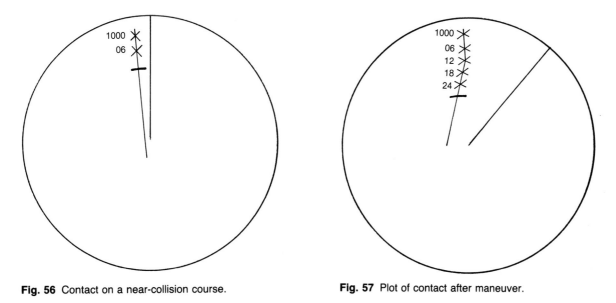

Fig. 56 Contact on a near-collision course.

Fig. 57 Plot of contact after maneuver.

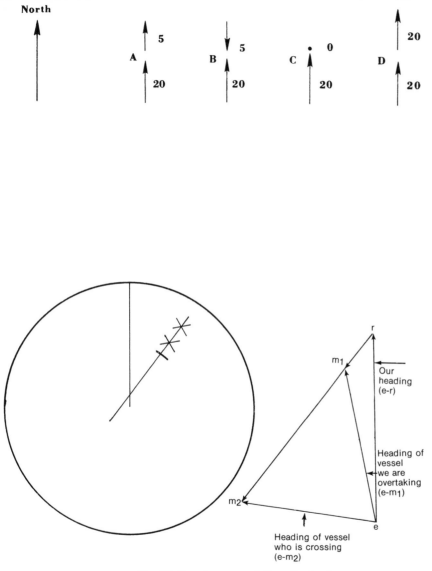

A 5 / 20

B 5 / 20

C 0 / 20

D 20 / 20

r
m₁

Our
heading
(e-r)

Heading of
vessel
we are
overtaking
(e-m₁)

m₂

e

Heading of vessel
who is crossing
(e-m₂)

Fig. 58 Crossing or overtaking situation?

course as our own vessel, on an opposite course, or dead in the water (DIW).

Consider the examples at top of this page, where our own vessel is headed north at 20 knots in each case.

In case A, the SRM is 15 knots (less than our own speed)—we are overtaking the other vessel. In case B, the SRM is 25 knots (greater than our own speed)—the vessels are meeting head-on. In case C, the SRM is 20 knots (equal to our own speed) and the other vessel is DIW. In case D, the SRM is zero. The contact would be tracked toward the center of the scope in cases A, B, and C. If the positions are marked at equal time intervals, an estimate of the situation can be made by noting the relative closing speed.

For situations where the contact is not dead ahead, a quick glance at the radar might be deceptive. Consider a radar contact whose relative plot is crossing from right to left, as in Figure 58. At first glance it appears to be a crossing situation. However, it could also be an overtaking situation. The vectors shown illustrate two possibilities for the scope presentation (standard maneuvering board labels are employed). The vector e-m₁ shows a contact whose heading is only slightly left of our own, and whose speed is slightly less than our own. The vector e-m₂ shows a vessel crossing nearly at a right angle to our own course. The SRM is necessary to distinguish between overtaking and crossing. Notice how the SRM is relatively low in the overtaking case and increases with a greater angle between the courses.

Using the principles discussed, study the radar pictures and determine the approach situation. In

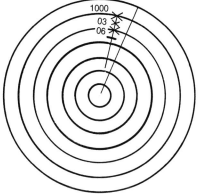

Fig. 59 Plot on radar scope.

all cases, our own vessel is proceeding at a speed of 16 knots and our heading is represented by the line projected from the center of the scope. Range circles are at one-mile intervals. Use the six-minute rule to determine SRM. Solutions are shown below each radar picture.

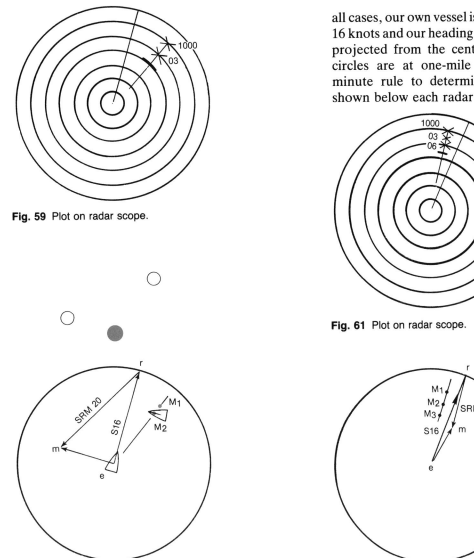

Fig. 60 Crossing situation. Aspects shown by lights above.

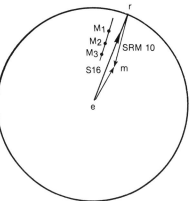

Fig. 61 Plot on radar scope.

Fig. 62 Overtaking situation. Sternlight only visible.

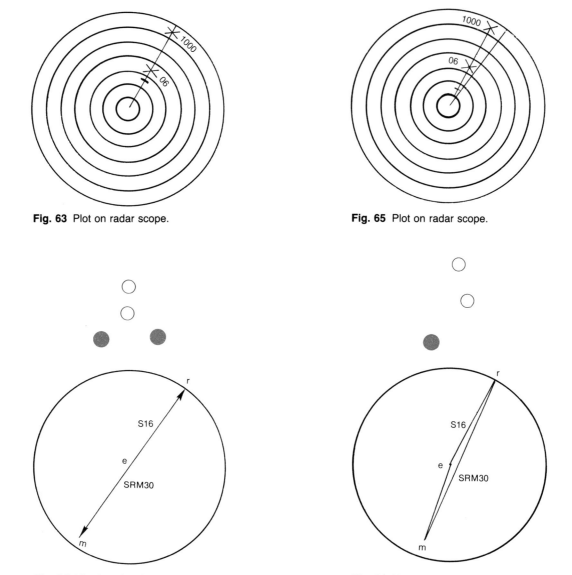

Fig. 63 Plot on radar scope.

Fig. 65 Plot on radar scope.

Fig. 64 Meeting situation. Aspect shown by lights above.

Fig. 66 Meeting situation. Aspect shown by lights above.

Appendices

A Bridge-to-Bridge Radiotelephone Log Requirements[1]

The log of the bridge-to-bridge station required by the Vessel Bridge-to-Bridge Radiotelephone Act shall include the following entries:

(1) All radiotelephone distress and alarm signals and communications transmitted or intercepted, the text in as complete form as possible of distress messages and distress communications, and any information connected with the radio service which may appear to be of importance to maritime safety, together with the time of such observation or occurrence, the frequencies used, and the position of the ship or other mobile unit in need of assistance if this can be determined.

(2) The times when the required watch is begun, interrupted, and ended. When the required watch is interrupted for any reason, the reason for such interruption shall be stated.

(3) A daily statement concerning the operating condition of the required radiotelephone equipment, as determined either by normal communication or test communication. Where the equipment is found not to comply with the applicable provisions of this part, the log shall contain a statement as to the time the condition was discovered and the time it was brought to the master's attention.

(4) Pertinent details of all installations, service, or maintenance work performed which may affect the proper operation of the station. The entry shall be made, signed, and dated by the responsible licensed operator who supervised or performed the work, and unless such operator is employed on a full-time basis and his operator license is properly posted at a station on board the ship, such entry shall include his mail address and the class, serial number, and expiration date of his operator license.

The bridge-to-bridge log may be part of the deck log or ship station log, or the log requirements may be satisfied by automated logging.

1. Title 47, Code of Federal Regulations, Section 83.368.

B Single-Letter Signals (Excerpt from H.O. 102)

May be made by any method of signaling.
See Note 1 for those marked by an asterisk (*)

A I have a diver down; keep well clear at slow speed.

*B I am taking in, or discharging, or carrying dangerous goods.

*C Yes (affirmative or "The significance of the previous group should be read in the affirmative").

*D Keep clear of me; I am maneuvering with difficulty.

*E I am altering my course to starboard.

F I am disabled; communicate with me.

*G I require a pilot. When made by fishing vessels operating in close proximity on the fishing grounds it means: "I am hauling nets."

*H I have a pilot on board.

*I I am altering my course to port.

J I am on fire and have dangerous cargo on board: keep well clear of me.

K I wish to communicate with you.[2]

L You should stop your vessel instantly.

M My vessel is stopped and making no way through the water.

N No (negative or "The significance of the previous group should be read in the negative"). This signal may be given only visually or by sound. For voice or radio transmission the signal should be **"NO."**

1. Signals of letters marked by an asterisk (*) when made by sound may only be made in compliance with the requirements of the International Regulations for Preventing Collisions at Sea, Rules **34** and **35**.

2. Signals "K" and "S" have special meanings as landing signals for small boats with crews or persons in distress. (International Convention for the Safety of Life at Sea, 1960, Chapter V, Regulations 16.)

O   **Man overboard.**

P   **In harbor.**—All persons should report on board as the vessel is about to proceed to sea. **At sea.**—It may be used by fishing vessels to mean: "My nets have come fast upon an obstruction."

Q   My vessel is "healthy" and I request free pratique.

*S   I am operating astern propulsion.[2]

*T   Keep clear of me; I am engaged in pair trawling.

U   You are running into danger.

V   I require assistance.

W   I require medical assistance.

X   Stop carrying out your intentions and watch for my signals.

Y   I am dragging my anchor.

*Z   I require a tug. When made by fishing vessels operating in close proximity on the fishing grounds it means: "I am shooting nets."

C Inland Navigational Rules Act of 1980 *and* International Regulations for Preventing Collisions at Sea, 1972

In order to save the reader a great deal of cross referencing, the COLREGS and Inland Rules are presented side by side with much of the duplication eliminated by indicating where the rules are the same. While differences in wording can make an important change in meaning, where differences in wording are merely editorial and do not change the meaning or requirements of the rules, it may be indicated that the rules are the same. A bar device has been placed in the margin to indicate those rules changed by the recent amendments to the COLREGS (effective 1 June 1983).

INLAND NAVIGATIONAL RULES ACT OF 1980

PART A—GENERAL

Rule 1

Application

    (a) These Rules apply to all vessels upon the inland waters of the United States, and to vessels of the United States on the Canadian waters of the Great Lakes to the extent that there is no conflict with Canadian law.

    (b) (i) These Rules constitute special rules made by an appropriate authority with-

INTERNATIONAL REGULATIONS FOR PREVENTING COLLISIONS AT SEA, 1972

PART A—GENERAL

Rule 1

Application

    (a) These rules shall apply to all vessels upon the high seas and in all waters connected therewith navigable by seagoing vessels.

    (b) Nothing in these rules shall interfere with the operation of special rules made by an appropriate authority for roadsteads, harbours, rivers, lakes or inland waterways in the meaning of Rule 1(b) of the International Regulations.

(ii) All vessels complying with the construction and equipment requirements of the International Regulations are considered to be in compliance with these Rules.

(c) Nothing in these Rules shall interfere with the operation of any special rules made by the Secretary of the Navy with respect to additional station or signal lights and shapes or whistle signals for ships of war and vessels proceeding under convoy, or by the Secretary with respect to additional station or signal lights and shapes for fishing vessels engaged in fishing as a fleet. These additional station or signal lights and shapes or whistle signals shall, so far as possible, be such that they cannot be mistaken for any light, shape, or signal authorized elsewhere under these Rules. Notice of such special rules shall be published in the Federal Register and, after the effective date specified in such notice, they shall have effect as if they were a part of these Rules.

(d) Vessel traffic service regulations may be in effect in certain areas.

(e) Whenever the Secretary determines that a vessel or class of vessels of special construction or purpose cannot comply fully with the provisions of any of these Rules with respect to the number, position, range, or arc of visibility of lights or shapes, as well as to the disposition and characteristics of

connected with the high seas and navigable by seagoing vessels. Such special rules shall conform as closely as possible to these rules.

(c) Nothing in these Rules shall interfere with the operation of any special rules made by the Government of any State with respect to additional station or signal lights, shapes or whistle signals for ships of war and vessels proceeding under convoy, or with respect to additional station or signal lights for fishing vessels engaged in fishing as a fleet. These additional station or signal lights, shapes, or whistle signals shall, so far as possible, be such that they cannot be mistaken for any light, shape or signal authorized elsewhere under these Rules.

(d) Traffic separation schemes may be adopted by the Organization for the purpose of these rules.

(e) Whenever the Government concerned shall have determined that a vessel of special construction or purpose cannot comply fully with the provisions of any of these rules with respect to the number, position, range or arc of visibility of lights or shapes, as well as to the disposition and characteristics of sound-signalling appliances, without interfering with the special function of the vessel, such vessel shall comply with such other provisions in regard to the number, position, range or arc of visibility of lights or shapes, as well as to the disposition and characteristics of sound-signalling appliances, as her Government shall have de-

sound-signaling appliances, without interfering with the special function of the vessel, the vessel shall comply with such other provisions in regard to the number, position, range, or arc of visibility of lights or shapes, as well as to the disposition and characteristics of sound-signaling appliances, as the Secretary shall have determined to be the closest possible compliance with these Rules. The Secretary may issue a certificate of alternative compliance for a vessel or class of vessels specifying the closest possible compliance with these Rules. The Secretary of the Navy shall make these determinations and issue certificates of alternative compliance for vessels of the Navy.

(f) The Secretary may accept a certificate of alternative compliance issued by a contracting party to the International Regulations if he determines that the alternative compliance standards of the contracting party are substantially the same as those of the United States.

Rule 2

Responsibility

(a) Nothing in these Rules shall exonerate any vessel, or the owner, master, or crew thereof, from the consequences of any neglect to comply with these Rules or of the neglect of any precaution which may be required by the ordinary practice of seamen, or by the special circumstances of the case.

termined to be the closest possible compliance with these rules in respect to that vessel.

Rule 2

Responsibility

Same as Inland

(b) In construing and complying with these Rules due regard shall be had to all dangers of navigation and collision and to any special circumstances, including the limitations of the vessels involved, which may make a departure from these Rules necessary to avoid immediate danger.

Rule 3

General Definitions

For the purpose of these Rules and this Act, except where the context otherwise requires:

(a) The word "vessel" includes every description of water craft, including nondisplacement craft and seaplanes, used or capable of being used as a means of transportation on water;

(b) The term "power-driven vessel" means any vessel propelled by machinery;

(c) The term "sailing vessel" means any vessel under sail provided that propelling machinery, if fitted, is not being used;

(d) The term "vessel engaged in fishing" means any vessel fishing with nets, lines, trawls, or other fishing apparatus which restricts maneuverability, but does not include a vessel fishing with trolling lines or other fishing apparatus which do not restrict maneuverability;

(e) The word "seaplane" includes any aircraft designed to maneuver on the water;

(f) The term "vessel not under command" means a vessel which through some exceptional circumstance is unable to maneuver as required by these Rules and is therefore

Rule 3

General Definitions

Definitions (a) through (g)—Same as Inland

unable to keep out of the way of another vessel;

(g) The term "vessel restricted in her ability to maneuver" means a vessel which from the nature of her work is restricted in her ability to maneuver as required by these Rules and is therefore unable to keep out of the way of another vessel; vessels restricted in their ability to maneuver include, but are not limited to:

   (i) a vessel engaged in laying, servicing, or picking up a navigation mark, submarine cable, or pipeline;

   (ii) a vessel engaged in dredging, surveying, or underwater operations;

   (iii) a vessel engaged in replenishment or transferring persons, provisions, or cargo while underway;

   (iv) a vessel engaged in the launching or recovery of aircraft;

   (v) a vessel engaged in minesweeping operations; and

   (vi) a vessel engaged in a towing operation such as severely restricts the towing vessel and her tow in their ability to deviate from their course.

(h) The word "underway" means that a vessel is not at anchor, or made fast to the shore, or aground;

(i) The words "length" and "breadth" of a vessel mean her length overall and greatest breadth;

(j) Vessels shall be deemed to be in sight of one another only when one can be observed visually from the other;

(h) through (k)—Same as Inland (but lettered differently)

(k) The term "restricted visibility" means any condition in which visibility is restricted by fog, mist, falling snow, heavy rainstorms, sandstorms, or any other similar causes;

(l) "Western Rivers" means the Mississippi River, its tributaries, South Pass, and Southwest Pass, to the navigational demarcation lines dividing the high seas from harbors, rivers, and other inland waters of the United States, and the Port Allen-Morgan City Alternate Route, and that part of the Atchafalaya River above its junction with the Port Allen-Morgan City Alternate Route including the Old River and the Red River;

(m) "Great Lakes" means the Great Lakes and their connecting and tributary waters including the Calumet River as far as the Thomas J. O'Brien Lock and Controlling Works (between mile 326 and 327), the Chicago River as far as the east side of the Ashland Avenue Bridge (between mile 321 and 322), and the Saint Lawrence River as far east as the lower exit of Saint Lambert Lock;

(n) "Secretary" means the Secretary of the department in which the Coast Guard is operating;

(o) "Inland Waters" means the navigable waters of the United States shoreward of the navigational demarcation lines dividing the high seas from harbors, rivers, and other inland waters of the United States and the waters of the Great Lakes on the United States side of the International Boundary;

(l) through (q)—Not in COLREGS

COLREGS Only:

The term "vessel constrained by her draught" means a power-driven vessel which because of her draught in relation to the available depth of water is severely restricted in her ability to deviate from the course she is following.

(p) "Inland Rules" or "Rules" mean the Inland Navigational Rules and the annexes thereto, which govern the conduct of vessels and specify the lights, shapes, and sound signals that apply on inland waters; and

(q) "International Regulations" means the International Regulations for Preventing Collisions at Sea, 1972, including annexes currently in force for the United States.

PART B—STEERING AND SAILING RULES
SUBPART I—CONDUCT OF VESSELS
IN ANY CONDITION OF VISIBILITY

Rule 4
Application
Rules in this subpart apply in any condition of visibility.

Rule 5
Look-out
Every vessel shall at all times maintain a proper look-out by sight and hearing as well as by all available means appropriate in the prevailing circumstances and conditions so as to make a full appraisal of the situation and of the risk of collision.

Rule 6
Safe Speed
Every vessel shall at all times proceed at a safe speed so that she can take proper and effective action to avoid collision and be stopped within a

PART B—STEERING AND SAILING RULES
SECTION I—CONDUCT OF VESSELS
IN ANY CONDITION OF VISIBILITY

Rule 4
Application
Rules in this Section apply in any condition of visibility.

Rule 5
Lookout
Same as Inland

Rule 6
Safe Speed
Same as Inland

distance appropriate to the prevailing circumstances and conditions.

In determining a safe speed the following factors shall be among those taken into account:

(a) By all vessels:
  (i) the state of visibility;
  (ii) the traffic density including concentration of fishing vessels or any other vessels;
  (iii) the maneuverability of the vessel with special reference to stopping distance and turning ability in the prevailing conditions;
  (iv) at night the presence of background light such as from shores lights or from back scatter of her own lights;
  (v) the state of wind, sea, and current, and the proximity of navigational hazards;
  (vi) the draft in relation to the available depth of water.

(b) Additionally, by vessels with operational radar:
  (i) the characteristics, efficiency and limitations of the radar equipment;
  (ii) any constraints imposed by the radar range scale in use;
  (iii) the effect on radar detection of the sea state, weather, and other sources of interference;
  (iv) the possibility that small vessels, ice and other floating objects may not be detected by radar at an adequate range;
  (v) the number, location, and movement of vessels detected by radar; and

(vi) the more exact assessment of the visibility that may be possible when radar is used to determine the range of vessels or other objects in the vicinity.

Rule 7
Risk of Collision
  (a) Every vessel shall use all available means appropriate to the prevailing circumstances and conditions to determine if risk of collision exists. If there is any doubt such risk shall be deemed to exist.
  (b) Proper use shall be made of radar equipment if fitted and operational, including long-range scanning to obtain early warning of risk of collision and radar plotting or equivalent systematic observation of detected objects.
  (c) Assumptions shall not be made on the basis of scanty information, especially scanty radar information.
  (d) In determining if risk of collision exists the following considerations shall be among those taken into account:
    (i) such risk shall be deemed to exist if the compass bearing of an approaching vessel does not appreciably change; and
    (ii) such risk may sometimes exist even when an appreciable bearing change is evident, particularly when approaching a very large vessel or a tow or when approaching a vessel at close range.

Rule 7
Risk of Collision
  Same as Inland

Rule 8

Action To Avoid Collision

(a) Any action taken to avoid collision shall, if the circumstances of the case admit, be positive, made in ample time and with due regard to the observance of good seamanship.

(b) Any alteration of course or speed to avoid collision shall, if the circumstances of the case admit, be large enough to be readily apparent to another vessel observing visually or by radar; a succession of small alterations of course or speed should be avoided.

(c) If there is sufficient sea room, alteration of course alone may be the most effective action to avoid a close-quarters situation provided that it is made in good time, is substantial and does not result in another close-quarters situation.

(d) Action taken to avoid collision with another vessel shall be such as to result in passing at a safe distance. The effectiveness of the action shall be carefully checked until the other vessel is finally past and clear.

(e) If necessary to avoid collision or allow more time to assess the situation, a vessel shall slacken her speed or take all way off by stopping or reversing her means of propulsion.

Rule 8

Action to Avoid Collision

Same as Inland

Rule 9

Narrow Channels

(a) (i) A vessel proceeding along the course of a narrow channel or fairway shall keep as near to the outer limit of the channel or fairway which lies on her starboard side as is safe and practicable.

(ii) Notwithstanding paragraph (a)(i) and Rule 14(a), a power-driven vessel operating in narrow channels or fairways on the Great Lakes, Western Rivers, or waters specified by the Secretary, and proceeding downbound with a following current shall have the right-of-way over an upbound vessel, shall propose the manner and place of passage, and shall initiate the maneuvering signals prescribed by Rule 34(a)(i), as appropriate. The vessel proceeding upbound against the current shall hold as necessary to permit safe passing.

(b) A vessel of less than 20 meters in length or a sailing vessel shall not impede the passage of a vessel that can safely navigate only within a narrow channel or fairway.

(c) A vessel engaged in fishing shall not impede the passage of any other vessel navigating within a narrow channel or fairway.

(d) A vessel shall not cross a narrow channel or fairway if such crossing impedes the passage of a vessel which can safely navigate only within that channel or fairway. The latter vessel shall use the danger signal pre-

Rule 9

Narrow Channels

(a) A vessel proceeding along the course of a narrow channel or fairway shall keep as near to the outer limit of the channel or fairway which lies on her starboard side as is safe and practicable.

(b) A vessel of less than 20 metres in length or a sailing vessel shall not impede the passage of a vessel which can safely navigate only within a narrow channel or fairway.

(c) A vessel engaged in fishing shall not impede the passage of any other vessel navigating within a narrow channel or fairway.

(d) A vessel shall not cross a narrow channel or fairway if such crossing impedes the passage of a vessel which can safely navigate only within such channel or fairway. The latter vessel may use the sound signal prescribed in Rule 34(d) if in doubt as to the intention of the crossing vessel.

(e) (i) In a narrow channel or fairway when overtaking can take place only if the vessel to be overtaken has to take action to permit safe passing, the vessel intending to overtake shall indicate her intention by sounding the appropriate signal prescribed in Rule 34(c)(i). The vessel to be overtaken shall, if in agreement, sound the appropriate signal prescribed in Rule 34(c)(ii) and take steps to permit safe passing. If in doubt she may sound the signals prescribed in Rule 34(d).

INLAND	COLREGS

<table>
<tr><td>

scribed in Rule 34(d) if in doubt as to the intention of the crossing vessel.

(e) (i) In a narrow channel or fairway when overtaking, the vessel intending to overtake shall indicate her intention by sounding the appropriate signal prescribed in Rule 34(c) and take steps to permit safe passing. The overtaken vessel, if in agreement, shall sound the same signal. If in doubt she shall sound the danger signal prescribed in Rule 34(d).

(ii) This Rule does not relieve the overtaking vessel of her obligation under Rule 13.

(f) A vessel nearing a bend or an area of a narrow channel or fairway where other vessels may be obscured by an intervening obstruction shall navigate with particular alertness and caution and shall sound the appropriate signal prescribed in Rule 34(e).

(g) Every vessel shall, if the circumstances of the case admit, avoid anchoring in a narrow channel.

</td><td>

(ii) This Rule does not relieve the overtaking vessel of her obligation under Rule 13.

(f) and (g)—Same as Inland

</td></tr>
</table>

Rule 10

Vessel Traffic Services

Each vessel required by regulation to participate in a vessel traffic service shall comply with the applicable regulations.

Rule 10

Traffic Separation Schemes

(a) This rule applies to traffic separation schemes adopted by the organization.

(b) A vessel using a traffic separation scheme shall:

(i) proceed in the appropriate traffic lane in the general direction of traffic flow for that lane;

(ii) so far as practicable keep clear of a traffic separation line or separation zone;

(iii) normally join or leave a traffic lane at the termination of the lane, but when joining or leaving from either side shall do so at as small an angle to the general direction of traffic flow as practicable.

(c) A vessel shall so far as practicable avoid crossing traffic lanes, but if obliged to do so shall cross as nearly as practicable at right angles to the general direction of traffic flow.

(d) Inshore traffic zones shall not normally be used by through traffic which can safely use the appropriate traffic lane within the adjacent traffic separation scheme. However vessels of less than 20 metres in length and sailing vessels may under all circumstances use inshore traffic zones.

(e) A vessel, other than a crossing vessel or a vessel joining or leaving a lane, shall not normally enter a separation zone or cross a separation line except:

(i) in cases of emergency to avoid immediate danger;

(ii) to engage in fishing within a separation zone.

(f) A vessel navigating in areas near the terminations of traffic separation schemes shall do so with particular caution.

(g) A vessel shall so far as practicable avoid anchoring in a traffic separation scheme or in areas near its terminations.

(h) A vessel not using a traffic separation

scheme shall avoid it by as wide a margin as is practicable.

(i) A vessel engaged in fishing shall not impede the passage of any vessel following a traffic lane.

(j) A vessel of less than 20 metres in length or a sailing vessel shall not impede the safe passage of a power-driven vessel following a traffic lane.

(k) A vessel restricted in her ability to manoeuvre when engaged in an operation for the maintenance of safety of navigation in a traffic separation scheme is exempted from complying with this Rule to the extent necessary to carry out the operation.

(l) A vessel restricted in her ability to manoeuvre when engaged in an operation for the laying, servicing or picking up of a submarine cable, within a traffic separation scheme, is exempted from complying with this Rule to the extent necessary to carry out the operation.

SUBPART II—CONDUCT OF VESSELS IN SIGHT OF ONE ANOTHER

Rule 11
Application
   Rules in this subpart apply to vessels in sight of one another.

Rule 12
Sailing Vessels
   (a) When two sailing vessels are approaching one another, so as to involve risk of colli-

SECTION II—CONDUCT OF VESSELS IN SIGHT OF ONE ANOTHER

Rule 11
Application
   Rules in this Section apply to vessels in sight of one another.

Rule 12
Sailing Vessels
   Same as Inland

sion, one of them shall keep out of the way of the other as follows:

(i) when each has the wind on a different side, the vessel which has the wind on the port side shall keep out of the way of the other;

(ii) when both have the wind on the same side, the vessel which is to windward shall keep out of the way of the vessel which is to leeward; and

(iii) if a vessel with the wind on the port side sees a vessel to windward and cannot determine with certainty whether the other vessel has the wind on the port or on the starboard side, she shall keep out of the way of the other.

(b) For the purpose of this Rule the windward side shall be deemed to be the side opposite to that on which the mainsail is carried or, in the case of a square-rigged vessel, the side opposite to that on which the largest fore-and-aft sail is carried.

Rule 13
Overtaking

(a) Notwithstanding anything contained in Rules 4 through 18, any vessel overtaking any other shall keep out of the way of the vessel being overtaken.

(b) A vessel shall be deemed to be overtaking when coming up with another vessel from a direction more than 22.5 degrees abaft her beam; that is, in such a position with reference to the vessel she is overtaking, that at night she would be able to see only the

Rule 13
Overtaking

(a) Notwithstanding anything contained in the Rules of Part B, Sections I and II any vessel overtaking any other shall keep out of the way of the vessel being overtaken.

(b), (c), and (d)—Same as Inland

sternlight of that vessel but neither of her sidelights.

(c) When a vessel is in any doubt as to whether she is overtaking another, she shall assume that this is the case and act accordingly.

(d) Any subsequent alteration of the bearing between the two vessels shall not make the overtaking vessel a crossing vessel within the meaning of these Rules or relieve her of the duty of keeping clear of the overtaken vessel until she is finally past and clear.

Rule 14

Head-On Situation

(a) When two power-driven vessels are meeting on reciprocal or nearly reciprocal courses so as to involve risk of collision each shall alter her course to starboard so that each shall pass on the port side of the other.

(b) Such a situation shall be deemed to exist when a vessel sees the other ahead or nearly ahead and by night she could see the masthead lights of the other in a line or nearly in a line or both sidelights and by day she observes the corresponding aspect of the other vessel.

(c) When a vessel is in any doubt as to whether such a situation exists she shall assume that it does exist and act accordingly.

Rule 15

Crossing Situation

(a) When two power-driven vessels are crossing so as to involve risk of collision, the vessel which has the other on her starboard

Rule 14

Head-On Situation
Same as Inland

Rule 15

Crossing Situation
 (a)—Same as Inland
 (b)—Applies only to Great Lakes and Western Rivers

side shall keep out of the way and shall, if the circumstances of the case admit, avoid crossing ahead of the other vessel.

(b) Notwithstanding paragraph (a), on the Great Lakes, Western Rivers, or water specified by the Secretary, a vessel crossing a river shall keep out of the way of a power-driven vessel ascending or descending the river.

Rule 16

Action by Give-Way Vessel

Every vessel which is directed to keep out of the way of another vessel shall, so far as possible, take early and substantial action to keep well clear.

Rule 17

Action by Stand-On Vessel

(a) (i) Where one of two vessels is to keep out of the way, the other shall keep her course and speed.

(ii) The latter vessel may, however, take action to avoid collision by her maneuver alone, as soon as it becomes apparent to her that the vessel required to keep out of the way is not taking appropriate action in compliance with these Rules.

(b) When, from any cause, the vessel required to keep her course and speed finds herself so close that collision cannot be avoided by the action of the give-way vessel alone, she shall take such action as will best aid to avoid collision.

(c) A power-driven vessel which takes action in a crossing situation in accordance with subparagraph (a)(ii) of this Rule to avoid

Rule 16

Action by Give-Way Vessel
Same as Inland

Rule 17

Action by Stand-On Vessel
Same as Inland

collision with another power-driven vessel shall, if the circumstances of the case admit, not alter course to port for a vessel on her own port side.

(d) This Rule does not relieve the give-way vessel of her obligation to keep out of the way.

Rule 18

Responsibilities Between Vessels

Except where Rules 9, 10, and 13 otherwise require:

(a) A power-driven vessel underway shall keep out of the way of:
   (i) a vessel not under command;
   (ii) a vessel restricted in her ability to maneuver;
   (iii) a vessel engaged in fishing; and
   (iv) a sailing vessel.

(b) A sailing vessel underway shall keep out of the way of:
   (i) a vessel not under command;
   (ii) a vessel restricted in her ability to maneuver; and
   (iii) a vessel engaged in fishing.

(c) A vessel engaged in fishing when underway shall, so far as possible, keep out of the way of:
   (i) a vessel not under command; and
   (ii) a vessel restricted in her ability to maneuver.

(d) A seaplane on the water shall, in general, keep well clear of all vessels and avoid impeding their navigation. In circumstances, however, where risk of collision exists, she shall comply with the Rules of this Part.

Rule 18

Responsibilities Between Vessels

Except where Rules 9, 10 and 13 otherwise require:

(a), (b), and (c)—Same as Inland

(d)—Same as Inland (but lettered differently)

COLREGS only:

(i) Any vessel other than a vessel not under command or a vessel restricted in her ability to manoeuvre shall, if the circumstances of the case admit, avoid impeding the safe passage of a vessel constrained by her draught, exhibiting the signals in Rule 28.

(ii) A vessel constrained by her draught shall navigate with particular caution having full regard to her special condition.

SUBPART III—CONDUCT OF VESSELS IN RESTRICTED VISIBILITY

SECTION III—CONDUCT OF VESSELS IN RESTRICTED VISIBILITY

Rule 19

Conduct of Vessels in Restricted Visibility

(a) This Rule applies to vessels not in sight of one another when navigating in or near an area of restricted visibility.

(b) Every vessel shall proceed at a safe speed adapted to the prevailing circumstances and conditions of restricted visibility. A power-driven vessel shall have her engines ready for immediate maneuver.

(c) Every vessel shall have due regard to the prevailing circumstances and conditions of restricted visibility when complying with Rules 4 through 10.

(d) A vessel which detects by radar alone the presence of another vessel shall determine if a close-quarters situation is developing or risk of collision exists. If so, she shall take avoiding action in ample time, provided that when such action consists of an alteration of course, so far as possible the following shall be avoided:

    (i) an alteration of course to port for a vessel forward of the beam, other than for a vessel being overtaken; and

    (ii) an alteration of course toward a vessel abeam or abaft the beam.

(e) Except where it has been determined that a risk of collision does not exist, every vessel which hears apparently forward of her beam the fog signal of another vessel, or

Rule 19

Conduct of Vessels in Restricted Visibility
    Same as Inland

which cannot avoid a close-quarters situation with another vessel forward of her beam, shall reduce her speed to the minimum at which she can be kept on course. She shall if necessary take all her way off and, in any event, navigate with extreme caution until danger of collision is over.

PART C—LIGHTS AND SHAPES

Rule 20
Application
    (a) Rules in this Part shall be complied with in all weathers.
    (b) The Rules concerning lights shall be complied with from sunset to sunrise, and during such times no other lights shall be exhibited, except such lights as cannot be mistaken for the lights specified in these Rules or do not impair their visibility or distinctive character, or interfere with the keeping of a proper lookout.
    (c) The lights prescribed by these Rules shall, if carried, also be exhibited from sunrise to sunset in restricted visibility and may be exhibited in all other circumstances when it is deemed necessary.
    (d) The Rules concerning shapes shall be complied with by day.
    (e) The lights and shapes specified in these Rules shall comply with the provisions of Annex I of these Rules.

PART C—LIGHTS AND SHAPES

Rule 20
Application
    Same as Inland

Rule 21

Definitions

(a) "Masthead light" means a white light placed over the fore and aft centerline of the vessel showing an unbroken light over an arc of the horizon of 225 degrees and so fixed as to show the light from right ahead to 22.5 degrees abaft the beam on either side of the vessel, except that on a vessel of less than 12 meters in length the masthead light shall be placed as nearly as practicable to the fore and aft centerline of the vessel.

(b) "Sidelights" mean a green light on the starboard side and a red light on the port side each showing an unbroken light over an arc of the horizon of 112.5 degrees and so fixed as to show the light from right ahead to 22.5 degrees abaft the beam on its respective side. On a vessel of less than 20 meters in length the side lights may be combined in one lantern carried on the fore and aft centerline of the vessel, except that on a vessel of less than 12 meters in length the sidelights when combined in one lantern shall be placed as nearly as practicable to the fore and aft centerline of the vessel.

(c) "Sternlight" means a white light placed as nearly as practicable at the stern showing an unbroken light over an arc of the horizon of 135 degrees and so fixed as to show the light 67.5 degrees from right aft on each side of the vessel.

(d) "Towing light" means a yellow light having the same characteristics as the "sternlight" defined in paragraph (c) of this Rule.

Rule 21

Definitions

(a) "Masthead light" means a white light placed over the fore and aft centreline of the vessel showing an unbroken light over an arc of the horizon of 225 degrees and so fixed as to show the light from right ahead to 22.5 degrees abaft the beam on either side of the vessel.

(b) "Sidelights" means a green light on the starboard side and a red light on the port side each showing an unbroken light over an arc of the horizon of 112.5 degrees and so fixed as to show the light from right ahead to 22.5 degrees abaft the beam on its respective side. In a vessel of less than 20 metres in length the sidelights may be combined in one lantern carried on the fore and aft centreline of the vessel.

(c), (d), (e), and (f)—Same as Inland

(g)—Not in the COLREGS

(e) "All-round light" means a light showing an unbroken light over an arc of the horizon of 360 degrees.

(f) "Flashing light" means a light flashing at regular intervals at a frequency of 120 flashes or more per minute.

(g) "Special flashing light" means a yellow light flashing at regular intervals at a frequency of 50 to 70 flashes per minute, placed as far forward and as nearly as practicable on the fore and aft centerline of the tow and showing an unbroken light over an arc of the horizon of not less than 180 degrees nor more than 225 degrees and so fixed as to show the light from right ahead to abeam and no more than 22.5 degrees abaft the beam on either side of the vessel.

Rule 22

Visibility of Lights

The lights prescribed in these Rules shall have an intensity as specified in Annex I to these Rules, so as to be visible at the following minimum ranges:

(a) In a vessel of 50 meters or more in length:
a masthead light, 6 miles;
a sidelight, 3 miles;
a sternlight, 3 miles;
a towing light, 3 miles;
a white, red, green or yellow all-round light, 3 miles; and
a special flashing light, 2 miles.

(b) In a vessel of 12 meters or more in length but less than 50 meters in length:

Rule 22

Visibility of Lights

The lights prescribed in these rules shall have an intensity as specified in Section 8 of Annex I to these regulations so as to be visible at the following minimum ranges:

(a) In vessels of 50 metres or more in length:
—a masthead light, 6 miles;
—a sidelight, 3 miles;
—a sternlight, 3 miles;
—a towing light, 3 miles;
—a white, red, green or yellow all-round light, 3 miles.

(b) In vessels of 12 metres or more in length but less than 50 metres in length:
—a masthead light, 5 miles; except that where

a masthead light, 5 miles; except that where the length of the vessel is less than 20 meters, 3 miles;
a sidelight, 2 miles;
a sternlight, 2 miles;
a towing light, 2 miles;
a white, red, green or yellow all-round light, 2 miles; and
a special flashing light, 2 miles.

(c) In a vessel of less than 12 meters in length:
a masthead light, 2 miles;
a sidelight, 1 mile;
a sternlight, 2 miles;
a towing light, 2 miles;
a white, red, green or yellow all-round light, 2 miles; and
a special flashing light, 2 miles.

(d) In an inconspicuous, partly submerged vessel or object being towed:
a white all-round light, 3 miles.

Rule 23

Power-Driven Vessels Underway

(a) A power-driven vessel underway shall exhibit:

  (i) a masthead light forward; except that a vessel of less than 20 meters in length need not exhibit this light forward of amidships but shall exhibit it as far forward as is practicable;

  (ii) a second masthead light abaft of and higher than the forward one; except that a vessel of less than 50 meters in length shall not be obliged to exhibit such light but may do so;

---

the length of the vessel is less than 20 metres, 3 miles;
—a sidelight, 2 miles;
—a sternlight, 2 miles;
—a towing light, 2 miles;
—a white, red, green, or yellow all-round light, 2 miles.

(c) In vessels of less than 12 metres in length:
—a masthead light, 2 miles;
—a sidelight, 1 mile;
—a sternlight, 2 miles;
—a towing light, 2 miles;
—a white, red, green or yellow all-round light, 2 miles.

(d)—Same as Inland

Rule 23

Power-Driven Vessels Underway

(a) A power-driven vessel underway shall exhibit:

  (i) a masthead light forward;

  (ii) a second masthead light abaft of and higher than the forward one; except that a vessel of less than 50 metres in length shall not be obliged to exhibit such light but may do so;

  (iii) sidelights;

  (iv) a sternlight.

(b) An air-cushion vessel when operating in the non-displacement mode shall, in addition

(iii) sidelights; and

(iv) a sternlight.

(b) An air-cushion vessel when operating in the nondisplacement mode shall, in addition to the lights prescribed in paragraph (a) of this Rule, exhibit an all-round flashing yellow light where it can best be seen.

(c) A power-driven vessel of less than 12 meters in length may, in lieu of the lights prescribed in paragraph (a) of this Rule, exhibit an all-round white light and sidelights.

(d) A power-driven vessel when operating on the Great Lakes may carry an all-round white light in lieu of the second masthead light and sternlight prescribed in paragraph (a) of this Rule. The light shall be carried in the position of the second masthead light and be visible at the same minimum range.

to the lights prescribed in paragraph (a) of this rule, exhibit an all-around flashing yellow light.

(c)(i)   A power-driven vessel of less than 12 metres in length may in lieu of the lights prescribed in paragraph (a) of this Rule exhibit an all-round white light and sidelights;

(ii) a power-driven vessel of less than 7 metres in length whose maximum speed does not exceed 7 knots may in lieu of the lights prescribed in paragraph (a) of this Rule exhibit an all-round white light and shall, if practicable, also exhibit sidelights;

(iii) the masthead light or all-round white light on a power-driven vessel of less than 12 metres in length may be displaced from the fore and aft centreline of the vessel if centreline fitting is not practicable, provided that the sidelights are combined in one lantern which shall be carried on the fore and aft centreline of the vessel or located as nearly as practicable in the same fore and aft line as the masthead light or the all-round white light.

Rule 24

Towing and Pushing

(a) A power-driven vessel when towing astern shall exhibit:

(i)   instead of the light prescribed either in Rule 23 (a)(i) or 23 (a)(ii), two mast-

Rule 24

Towing and Pushing

(a) and (b)—Same as Inland

head lights in a vertical line. When the
length of the tow, measuring from the
stern of the towing vessel to the after
end of the tow exceeds 200 meters,
three such lights in a vertical line;

(ii) sidelights;

(iii) a sternlight;

(iv) a towing light in a vertical line above
the sternlight; and

(v) when the length of the tow exceeds 200
meters, a diamond shape where it can
best be seen.

(b) When a pushing vessel and a vessel being
pushed ahead are rigidly connected in a
composite unit they shall be regarded as a
power-driven vessel and exhibit the lights
prescribed in Rule 23.

(c) A power-driven vessel when pushing ahead
or towing alongside, except as required by
paragraphs (b) and (i) of this Rule, shall
exhibit:

(i) instead of the light prescribed either in
Rule 23(a)(i) or 23(a)(ii), two masthead lights in a vertical line;

(ii) sidelights; and

(iii) two towing lights in a vertical line.

(d) A power-driven vessel to which paragraphs
(a) or (c) of this Rule apply shall also comply with Rule 23 (a)(i) and 23(a)(ii).

(e) A vessel or object other than those referred
to in paragraph (g) of this Rule being towed
shall exhibit:

(i) sidelights;

(ii) a sternlight; and

(iii) when the length of the tow exceeds 200

(c) A power-driven vessel when pushing ahead
or towing alongside, except in the case of a
composite unit, shall exhibit:

(i) instead of the light prescribed in Rule
23(a)(i) or (ii), two masthead lights in
a vertical line;

(ii) sidelights;

(iii) a sternlight.

(d) A power-driven vessel to which paragraph
(a) or (c) of this rule apply shall also comply
with Rule 23(a)(ii).

(e)—Same as Inland

meters, a diamond shape where it can best be seen.

(f) Provided that any number of vessels being towed alongside or pushed in a group shall be lighted as one vessel:

 (i) a vessel being pushed ahead, not being part of a composite unit, shall exhibit at the forward end sidelights, and a special flashing light; and

 (ii) a vessel being towed alongside shall exhibit a sternlight and at the forward end sidelights.

(g) An inconspicuous, partly submerged vessel or object being towed shall exhibit:

 (i) if it is less than 25 meters in breadth, one all-round white light at or near each end;

 (ii) if it is 25 meters or more in breadth, four all-round white lights to mark its length and breadth;

 (iii) if it exceeds 100 meters in length, additional all-round white lights between the lights prescribed in subparagraphs (i) and (ii) so that the distance between the lights shall not exceed 100 meters: *Provided*, That any vessels or objects being towed alongside each other shall be lighted as one vessel or object;

 (iv) a diamond shape at or near the aftermost extremity of the last vessel or object being towed; and

 (v) the towing vessel may direct a searchlight in the direction of the tow to indicate its presence to an approaching vessel.

(f) Provided that any number of vessels being towed alongside or pushed in a group shall be lighted as one vessel,

 (i) a vessel being pushed ahead, not being part of a composite unit, shall exhibit at the forward end, sidelights;

 (ii) a vessel being towed alongside shall exhibit a sternlight and at the forward end, sidelights.

(g) An inconspicuous, partly submerged vessel or object, or combination of such vessels or objects being towed shall exhibit:

 (i) if it is less than 25 metres in breadth, one all-round white light at or near the forward end and one at or near the after end except that dracones need not exhibit a light at or near the forward end;

 (ii) if it is 25 metres or more in breadth, two additional all-round white lights at or near the extremities of its breadth;

 (iii) if it exceeds 100 metres in length, additional all-round white lights between the lights prescribed in sub-paragraphs (i) and (ii) so that the distance between the lights shall not exceed 100 metres;

 (iv) a diamond shape at or near the aftermost extremity of the last vessel or object being towed and if the length of the tow exceeds 200 metres an additional diamond shape where it can best be seen and located as far forward as is practicable.

(h) Where from any sufficient cause it is impracticable for a vessel or object being towed to exhibit the lights prescribed in paragraph (e) or (g) of this Rule, all possible measures shall be taken to light the vessel or object towed or at least to indicate the presence of the unlighted vessel or object.

(h)—Same as Inland

(i) Notwithstanding paragraph (c), on the Western Rivers and on waters specified by the Secretary, a power-driven vessel when pushing ahead or towing alongside, except as paragraph (b) applies, shall exhibit:
   (i) sidelights; and
   (ii) two towing lights in a vertical line.

(i) —Not in COLREGS

(j) Where from any sufficient cause it is impracticable for a vessel not normally engaged in towing operations to display the lights prescribed by paragraph (a), (c) or (i) of this Rule, such vessel shall not be required to exhibit those lights when engaged in towing another vessel in distress or otherwise in need of assistance. All possible measures shall be taken to indicate the nature of the relationship between the towing vessel and the vessel being assisted. The searchlight authorized by Rule 36 may be used to illuminate the tow.

(j)—Same as Inland, but lettered differently

Rule 25
Sailing Vessels Underway and Vessels Under Oars
  (a) A sailing vessel underway shall exhibit:
    (i) sidelights; and
    (ii) a sternlight.
  (b) In a sailing vessel of less than 20 meters in length the lights prescribed in paragraph

Rule 25
Sailing Vessels Underway and Vessels Under Oars
  (a) through (c)—Same as Inland

(a) of this Rule may be combined in one lantern carried at or near the top of the mast where it can best be seen.

(c) A sailing vessel underway may, in addition to the lights prescribed in paragraph (a) of this Rule, exhibit at or near the top of the mast, where they can best be seen, two all-round lights in a vertical line, the upper being red and the lower green, but these lights shall not be exhibited in conjunction with the combined lantern permitted by paragraph (b) of this Rule.

(d) (i) A sailing vessel of less than 7 meters in length shall, if practicable, exhibit the lights prescribed in paragraph (a) or (b) of this Rule, but if she does not, she shall have ready at hand an electric torch or lighted lantern showing a white light which shall be exhibited in sufficient time to prevent collision.

(ii) A vessel under oars may exhibit the lights prescribed in this Rule for sailing vessels, but if she does not, she shall have ready at hand an electric torch or lighted lantern showing a white light which shall be exhibited in sufficient time to prevent collision.

(d)—Same as Inland

(e) A vessel proceeding under sail when also being propelled by machinery shall exhibit forward where it can best be seen a conical shape, apex downward. A vessel of less than 12 meters in length is not required to exhibit this shape, but may do so.

(e) A vessel proceeding under sail when also being propelled by machinery shall exhibit forward where it can best be seen a conical shape, apex downwards.

Rule 26   **Rule 26**

Fishing Vessels   *Fishing Vessels*

    (a) A vessel engaged in fishing, whether under-   Same as Inland
way or at anchor, shall exhibit only the
lights and shapes prescribed in this Rule.

    (b) A vessel when engaged in trawling, by
which is meant the dragging through the
water of a dredge net or other apparatus
used as a fishing appliance, shall exhibit:

        (i)   two all-round lights in a vertical line,
the upper being green and the lower
white, or a shape consisting of two
cones with their apexes together in a
vertical line one above the other; a
vessel of less than 20 meters in length
may instead of this shape exhibit a
basket;

        (ii) a masthead light abaft of and higher
than the all-round green light; a vessel
of less than 50 meters in length shall
not be obliged to exhibit such a light
but may do so; and

        (iii) when making way through the water,
in addition to the lights prescribed in
this paragraph, sidelights and a sternlight.

    (c) A vessel engaged in fishing, other than
trawling, shall exhibit:

        (i)   two all-round lights in a vertical line,
the upper being red and the lower
white, or a shape consisting of two
cones with apexes together in a vertical line one above the other; a vessel of
less than 20 meters in length may instead of this shape exhibit a basket;

(ii) when there is outlying gear extending more than 150 meters horizontally from the vessel, an all-round white light or a cone apex upward in the direction of the gear; and

(iii) when making way through the water, in addition to the lights prescribed in this paragraph, sidelights and a sternlight.

(d) A vessel engaged in fishing in close proximity to other vessels engaged in fishing may exhibit the additional signals described in Annex II to these Rules.

(e) A vessel when not engaged in fishing shall not exhibit the lights or shapes prescribed in this Rule, but only those prescribed for a vessel of her length.

Rule 27

Vessels Not Under Command or Restricted in their Ability to Maneuver

(a) A vessel not under command shall exhibit:

(i) two all-round red lights in a vertical line where they can best be seen;

(ii) two balls or similar shapes in a vertical line where they can best be seen; and

(iii) when making way through the water, in addition to the lights prescribed in this paragraph, sidelights and a sternlight.

(b) A vessel restricted in her ability to maneuver, except a vessel engaged in minesweeping operations, shall exhibit:

(i) three all-round lights in a vertical line where they can best be seen. The high-

Rule 27

Vessels Not Under Command or Restricted in their Ability to Manoeuvre

(a) through (e)—Same as Inland

est and lowest of these lights shall be red and the middle light shall be white;

(ii) three shapes in a vertical line where they can best be seen. The highest and lowest of these shapes shall be balls and the middle one a diamond;

(iii) when making way through the water, masthead lights, sidelights and a sternlight, in addition to the lights prescribed in subparagraph (b)(i); and

(iv) when at anchor, in addition to the lights or shapes prescribed in subparagraphs (b) (i) and (ii), the light, lights or shapes prescribed in Rule 30.

(c) A vessel engaged in a towing operation which severely restricts the towing vessel and her tow in their ability to deviate from their course shall, in addition to the lights or shapes prescribed in subparagraphs (b) (i) and (ii) of this Rule, exhibit the lights or shape prescribed in Rule 24.

(d) A vessel engaged in dredging or underwater operations, when restricted in her ability to maneuver, shall exhibit the lights and shapes prescribed in subparagraphs (b) (i), (ii), and (iii) of this Rule and shall in addition, when an obstruction exists, exhibit:

(i) two all-round red lights or two balls in a vertical line to indicate the side on which the obstruction exists;

(ii) two all-round green lights or two diamonds in a vertical line to indicate the side on which another vessel may pass; and

(iii) when at anchor, the lights or shape prescribed by this paragraph, instead of the lights or shapes prescribed in Rule 30 for anchored vessels.

(e) Whenever the size of a vessel engaged in diving operations makes it impracticable to exhibit all lights and shapes prescribed in paragraph (d) of this Rule, the following shall instead be exhibited:

(i) Three all-round lights in a vertical line where they can best be seen. The highest and lowest of these lights shall be red and the middle light shall be white.

(ii) A rigid replica of the international Code flag "A" not less than 1 meter in height. Measures shall be taken to insure its all-round visibility.

(f) A vessel engaged in minesweeping operations shall, in addition to the lights prescribed for a power-driven vessel in Rule 23, exhibit three all-round green lights or three balls. One of these lights or shapes shall be exhibited near the foremast head and one at each end of the fore yard. These lights or shapes indicate that it is dangerous for another vessel to approach closer than 1,000 meters astern or 500 meters on either side of the minesweeper.

(g) A vessel of less than 12 meters in length, except when engaged in diving operations, is not required to exhibit the lights or shapes prescribed in this Rule.

(h) The signals prescribed in this Rule are not signals of vessels in distress and requiring assistance. Such signals are contained in Annex IV to these Rules.

(f) A vessel engaged in mine clearance operations shall in addition to the lights prescribed for a power-driven vessel in Rule 23 or to the lights or shape prescribed for a vessel at anchor in Rule 30 as appropriate, exhibit three all-round green lights or three balls. One of these lights or shapes shall be exhibited near the foremast head and one at each end of the fore yard. These lights and shapes indicate that it is dangerous for another vessel to approach within 1000 metres of the mine clearance vessel.

(g) and (h)—Same as Inland

INLAND	COLREGS
Rule 28 [Reserved]	**Rule 28** *Vessels Constrained by their Draught* A vessel constrained by her draught may, in addition to the lights prescribed for power-driven vessels in Rule 23, exhibit where they can best be seen three all-round red lights in a vertical line, or a cylinder.

Rule 29

Pilot Vessels

    (a) A vessel engaged on pilotage duty shall exhibit:

        (i)   at or near the masthead, two all-round lights in a vertical line, the upper being white and the lower red;

        (ii) when underway, in addition, side-lights and a sternlight; and

        (iii) when at anchor, in addition to the lights prescribed in subparagraph (i), the anchor light, lights, or shape prescribed in Rule 30 for anchored vessels.

    (b) A pilot vessel when not engaged on pilotage duty shall exhibit the lights or shapes prescribed for a vessel of her length.

Rule 29

Pilot Vessels

    Same as Inland

Rule 30

Anchored Vessels and Vessels Aground

    (a) A vessel at anchor shall exhibit where it can best be seen:

        (i) in the fore part, an all-round white light or one ball; and

        (ii) at or near the stern and at a lower level than the light prescribed in subparagraph (i), an all-round white light.

    (b) A vessel of less than 50 meters in length may exhibit an all-round white light where

Rule 30

Anchored Vessels and Vessels Aground

    (a) through (f)—Same as Inland

it can best be seen instead of the lights prescribed in paragraph (a) of this Rule.

(c) A vessel at anchor may, and a vessel of 100 meters or more in length shall, also use the available working or equivalent lights to illuminate her decks.

(d) A vessel aground shall exhibit the lights prescribed in paragraph (a) or (b) of this Rule and in addition, if practicable, where they can best be seen:
  (i) two all-round red lights in a vertical line; and
  (ii) three balls in a vertical line.

(e) A vessel of less than 7 meters in length, when at anchor, not in or near a narrow channel, fairway, anchorage, or where other vessels normally navigate, shall not be required to exhibit the lights or shape prescribed in paragraphs (a) and (b) of this Rule.

(f) A vessel of less than 12 meters in length when aground shall not be required to exhibit the lights or shapes prescribed in subparagraphs (d)(i) and (ii) of this Rule.

(g) A vessel of less than 20 meters in length, when at anchor in a special anchorage area designated by the Secretary, shall not be required to exhibit the anchor lights and shapes required by this Rule.

(g)—not in COLREGS

Rule 31
Seaplanes

Where it is impracticable for a seaplane to exhibit lights and shapes of the characteristics or in the positions prescribed in the Rules of this Part she shall exhibit lights and shapes as closely similar in characteristics and position as is possible.

Rule 31
Seaplanes
  Same as Inland

PART D—SOUND AND LIGHT SIGNALS

Rule 32
Definitions
- (a) The word "whistle" means any sound signaling appliance capable of producing the prescribed blasts and which complies with specifications in Annex III to these Rules.
- (b) The term "short blast" means a blast of about 1 second's duration.
- (c) The term "prolonged blast" means a blast of from 4 to 6 seconds' duration.

Rule 33
Equipment for Sound Signals
- (a) A vessel of 12 meters or more in length shall be provided with a whistle and a bell and a vessel of 100 meters or more in length shall, in addition, be provided with a gong, the tone and sound of which cannot be confused with that of the bell. The whistle, bell and gong shall comply with the specifications in Annex III to these Rules. The bell or gong or both may be replaced by other equipment having the same respective sound characteristics, provided that manual sounding of the prescribed signals shall always be possible.
- (b) A vessel of less than 12 meters in length shall not be obliged to carry the sound signaling appliances prescribed in paragraph (a) of this Rule but if she does not, she shall be provided with some other means of making an efficient sound signal.

PART D—SOUND AND LIGHT SIGNALS

Rule 32
Definitions
Same as Inland

Rule 33
Equipment for Sound Signals
Same as Inland

INLAND

Rule 34

Maneuvering and Warning Signals

(a) When power-driven vessels are in sight of one another and meeting or crossing at a distance within half a mile of each other, each vessel underway, when maneuvering as authorized or required by these Rules:

    (i) shall indicate that maneuver by the following signals on her whistle: one short blast to mean "I intend to leave you on my port side"; two short blasts to mean "I intend to leave you on my starboard side"; and three short blasts to mean "I am operating astern propulsion."

    (ii) upon hearing the one or two blast signal of the other shall, if in agreement, sound the same whistle signal and take the steps necessary to effect a safe passing. If, however, from any cause, the vessel doubts the safety of the proposed maneuver, she shall sound the danger signal specified in paragraph (d) of this Rule and each vessel shall take appropriate precautionary action until a safe passing agreement is made.

(b) A vessel may supplement the whistle signals prescribed in paragraph (a) of this Rule by light signals:

    (i) These signals shall have the following significance: one flash to mean "I intend to leave you on my port side"; two flashes to mean "I intend to leave you on my starboard side"; three flashes to mean "I am operating astern propulsion";

COLREGS

Rule 34

Manoeuvring and Warning Signals

(a) When vessels are in sight of one another, a power-driven vessel underway, when manoeuvring as authorized or required by these rules, shall indicate that manoeuvre by the following signals on her whistle:
—one short blast to mean "I am altering my course to starboard";
—two short blasts to mean "I am altering my course to port";
—three short blasts to mean "I am operating astern propulsion".

(b) Any vessel may supplement the whistle signals prescribed in paragraph (a) of this rule by light signals, repeated as appropriate, whilst the manoeuvre is being carried out.

    (i) these light signals shall have the following significance:
—one flash to mean "I am altering my course to starboard";
—two flashes to mean "I am altering my course to port";
—three flashes to mean "I am operating astern propulsion";

    (ii) the duration of each flash shall be about one second, the interval between flashes shall be about one second, and the interval between successive signals shall be not less than ten seconds;

    (iii) the light used for this signal shall, if fitted, be an all-round white light, visible at a minimum range of 5 miles, and shall comply with the provisions of Annex I to these Regulations.

(ii) The duration of each flash shall be about 1 second; and

(iii) The light used for this signal shall, if fitted, be one all-round white or yellow light, visible at a minimum range of 2 miles, synchronized with the whistle, and shall comply with the provisions of Annex I to these Rules.

(c) When in sight of one another:

(i) a power-driven vessel intending to overtake another power-driven vessel shall indicate her intention by the following signals on her whistle: one short blast to mean "I intend to overtake you on your starboard side"; two short blasts to mean "I intend to overtake you on your port side"; and

(ii) the power-driven vessel about to be overtaken shall, if in agreement, sound a similar sound signal. If in doubt she shall sound the danger signal prescribed in paragraph (d).

(d) When vessels in sight of one another are approaching each other and from any cause either vessel fails to understand the intentions or actions of the other, or is in doubt whether sufficient action is being taken by the other to avoid collision, the vessel in doubt shall immediately indicate such doubt by giving at least five short and rapid blasts on the whistle. This signal may be supplemented by a light signal of at least five short and rapid flashes.

(e) A vessel nearing a bend or an area of a channel or fairway where other vessels may

(c) When in sight of one another in a narrow channel or fairway:

(i) a vessel intending to overtake another shall in compliance with Rule 9(e)(i) indicate her intention by the following signals on her whistle:

—two prolonged blasts followed by one short blast to mean "I intend to overtake you on your starboard side";

—two prolonged blasts followed by two short blasts to mean "I intend to overtake you on your port side."

(ii) the vessel about to be overtaken when acting in accordance with Rule 9(e)(i) shall indicate her agreement by the following signal on her whistle:

—one prolonged, one short, one prolonged and one short blast, in that order.

(d), (e), and (f)—Same as Inland

(g)—Not in COLREGS

(h)—Not in COLREGS

be obscured by an intervening obstruction shall sound one prolonged blast. This signal shall be answered with a prolonged blast by any approaching vessel that may be within hearing around the bend or behind the intervening obstruction.

(f) If whistles are fitted on a vessel at a distance apart of more than 100 meters, one whistle only shall be used for giving maneuvering and warning signals.

(g) When a power-driven vessel is leaving a dock or berth, she shall sound one prolonged blast.

(h) A vessel that reaches agreement with another vessel in a meeting, crossing, or overtaking situation by using the radiotelephone as prescribed by the Bridge-to-Bridge Radiotelephone Act (85 Stat. 165; 33 U.S.C. 1207), is not obliged to sound the whistle signals prescribed by this Rule, but may do so. If agreement is not reached, then whistle signals shall be exchanged in a timely manner and shall prevail.

Rule 35

Sound Signals in Restricted Visibility

In or near an area of restricted visibility, whether by day or night, the signals prescribed in this Rule shall be used as follows:

(a) A power-driven vessel making way through the water shall sound at intervals of not more than 2 minutes one prolonged blast.

(b) A power-driven vessel underway but stopped and making no way through the

Rule 35

Sound Signals in Restricted Visibility

In or near an area of restricted visibility, whether by day or night, the signals prescribed in this rule shall be used as follows:

(a) and (b)—Same as Inland

(c) A vessel not under command, a vessel restricted in her ability to manoeuvre, a vessel constrained by her draught, a sailing vessel, a vessel engaged in fishing and a

INLAND

water shall sound at intervals of not more than 2 minutes two prolonged blasts in succession with an interval of about 2 seconds between them.

(c) A vessel not under command; a vessel restricted in her ability to maneuver, whether underway or at anchor; a sailing vessel; a vessel engaged in fishing, whether underway or at anchor; and a vessel engaged in towing or pushing another vessel shall, instead of the signals prescribed in paragraphs (a) or (b) of this Rule, sound at intervals of not more than 2 minutes, three blasts in succession; namely, one prolonged followed by two short blasts.

(d) A vessel towed or if more than one vessel is towed the last vessel of the tow, if manned, shall at intervals of not more than 2 minutes sound four blasts in succession; namely, one prolonged followed by three short blasts. When practicable, this signal shall be made immediately after the signal made by the towing vessel.

(e) When a pushing vessel and a vessel being pushed ahead are rigidly connected in a composite unit they shall be regarded as a power-driven vessel and shall give the signals prescribed in paragraphs (a) or (b) of this Rule.

(f) A vessel at anchor shall at intervals of not more than 1 minute ring the bell rapidly for about 5 seconds. In a vessel of 100 meters or more in length the bell shall be sounded in the forepart of the vessel and immediately after the ringing of the bell the gong shall be

COLREGS

vessel engaged in towing or pushing another vessel shall, instead of the signals prescribed in paragraphs (a) or (b) of this rule, sound at intervals of not more than 2 minutes three blasts in succession, namely one prolonged followed by two short blasts.

(d) through (i)—Same as Inland

sounded rapidly for about 5 seconds in the after part of the vessel. A vessel at anchor may in addition sound three blasts in succession; namely, one short, one prolonged and one short blast, to give warning of her position and of the possibility of collision to an approaching vessel.

(g) A vessel aground shall give the bell signal and if required the gong signal prescribed in paragraph (f) of this Rule and shall, in addition, give three separate and distinct strokes on the bell immediately before and after the rapid ringing of the bell. A vessel aground may in addition sound an appropriate whistle signal.

(h) A vessel of less than 12 meters in length shall not be obliged to give the above-mentioned signals but, if she does not, shall make some other efficient sound signal at intervals of not more than 2 minutes.

(i) A pilot vessel when engaged on pilotage duty may in addition to the signals prescribed in paragraphs (a), (b) or (f) of this Rule sound an identity signal consisting of four short blasts.

(j) The following vessels shall not be required to sound signals as prescribed in paragraph (f) of this Rule when anchored in a special anchorage area designated by the Secretary:

    (i) a vessel of less than 20 meters in length; and

    (ii) a barge, canal boat, scow, or other nondescript craft.

(j)—Not in COLREGS

Rule 36
Signals To Attract Attention

If necessary to attract the attention of another vessel, any vessel may make light or sound signals that cannot be mistaken for any signal authorized elsewhere in these Rules, or may direct the beam of her searchlight in the direction of the danger, in such a way as not to embarrass any vessel.

Rule 37
Distress Signals

When a vessel is in distress and requires assistance she shall use or exhibit the signals described in Annex IV to these Rules.

PART E—EXEMPTIONS

Rule 38
Exemptions

Any vessel or class of vessels, the keel of which is laid or which is at a corresponding stage of construction before the date of enactment of this Act, provided that she complies with the requirements of—

(a) The Act of June 7, 1897 (30 Stat. 96), as amended (33 U.S.C. 154–232) for vessels navigating the waters subject to that statute;

(b) Section 4233 of the Revised Statutes (33 U.S.C. 301–356) for vessels navigating the waters subject to that statute;

(c) The Act of February 8, 1895 (28 Stat. 645), as amended (33 U.S.C. 241–295) for vessels navigating the waters subject to that statute; or

Rule 36
Signals to Attract Attention

Same as Inland except for following:

Any light to attract the attention of another vessel shall be such that it cannot be mistaken for any aid to navigation. For the purpose of this rule the use of high intensity intermittent or revolving lights, such as strobe lights, shall be avoided.

[Note: this provision may be deleted if a sufficient number of countries object.]

Rule 37
Distress Signals

Same as Inland

PART E—EXEMPTIONS

Rule 38
Exemptions

Any vessel (or class of vessels) provided that she complies with the requirements of the International Regulations for Preventing Collisions at Sea, 1960, the keel of which is laid or which is at a corresponding stage of construction before the entry into force of these regulations may be exempted from compliance therewith as follows:

(a) The installation of lights with ranges prescribed in Rule 22, until four years after the date of entry into force of these regulations.

(b) The installation of lights with colour specifications as prescribed in Section 7 of Annex I to these regulations, until four years after the date of entry into force of these regulations.

(c) The repositioning of lights as a result of

(d) Sections 3, 4, and 5 of the Act of April 25, 1940 (54 Stat. 163), as amended (46 U.S.C. 526 b, c, and d) for motorboats navigating the waters subject to that statute; shall be exempted from compliance with the technical Annexes to these Rules as follows:

(i)   the installation of lights with ranges prescribed in Rule 22, until 4 years after the effective date of these Rules, except that vessels of less than 20 meters in length are permanently exempt;

(ii)   the installation of lights with color specifications as prescribed in Annex I to these Rules, until 4 years after the effective date of these Rules, except that vessels of less than 20 meters in length are permanently exempt;

(iii) the repositioning of lights as a result of conversion to metric units and rounding off measurement figures, are permanently exempt; and

(iv)   the horizontal repositioning of masthead lights prescribed by Annex I to these Rules:

(1) on vessels of less than 150 meters in length, permanent exemption.

(2) on vessels of 150 meters or more in length, until 9 years after the effective date of these Rules.

(v)   the restructuring or repositioning of all lights to meet the prescriptions of Annex I to these Rules, until 9 years after the effective date of these Rules;

conversion from Imperial to metric units and rounding off measurement figures, permanent exemption.

(d) (i)   The repositioning of masthead lights on vessels of less than 150 metres in length, resulting from the prescriptions of Section 3(a) of Annex I to these Regulations, permanent exemption.

(ii) The repositioning of masthead lights on vessels of 150 metres or more in length, resulting from the prescriptions of Section 3(a) of Annex I to these regulations, until 9 years after the date of entry into force of these regulations.

(e) The repositioning of masthead lights resulting from the prescriptions of Section 2(b) of Annex I to these Regulations, until 9 years after the date of entry into force of these regulations.

(f) The repositioning of sidelights resulting from the prescriptions of Sections 2(g) and 3(b) of Annex I to these Regulations, until 9 years after the date of entry into force of these regulations.

(g) The requirements for sound signal appliances prescribed in Annex III to these Regulations, until 9 years after the date of entry into force of these regulations.

(h) The repositioning of all-round lights resulting from the prescription of Section 9(b), of Annex I to these Regulations, permanent exemption.

(vi) power-driven vessels of 12 meters or more but less than 20 meters in length are permanently exempt from the provisions of Rule 23(a)(i) and 23(a)(iv) provided that, in place of these lights, the vessel exhibits a white light aft visible all round the horizon; and

(vii) the requirements for sound signal appliances prescribed in Annex III to these Rules, until 9 years after the effective date of these Rules.

ANNEX I

POSITIONING AND TECHNICAL DETAILS OF LIGHTS AND SHAPES

§ 84.01 *Definitions*

(a) The term "height above the hull" means height above the uppermost continuous deck. This height shall be measured from the position vertically beneath the location of the light.

(b) The term "practical cut-off" means, for vessels 20 meters or more in length, 12.5 percent of the minimum luminous intensity (Table 84.15(b)) corresponding to the greatest range of visibility for which the requirements of Annex I are met.

(c) The term "Rule" or "Rules" means the Inland Navigation Rules contained in sec. 2 of the Inland Navigational Rules Act of 1980 (Pub. L. 96–591, 94 Stat. 3415, 33 U.S.C. 2001, December 24, 1980) as amended.

ANNEX I

POSITIONING AND TECHNICAL DETAILS OF LIGHTS AND SHAPES

1. *Definition*

The term "height above the hull" means height above the uppermost continuous deck. This height shall be measured from the position vertically beneath the location of the light.

§ 84.03 *Vertical positioning and spacing of lights*

(a) On a power-driven vessel of 20 meters or more in length the masthead lights shall be placed as follows:

(1) The forward masthead light, or if only one masthead light is carried, then that light, at a height above the hull of not less than 5 meters, and, if the breadth of the vessel exceeds 5 meters, then at a height above the hull not less than such breadth, so however that the light need not be placed at a greater height above the hull than 8 meters;

(2) When two masthead lights are carried the after one shall be at least 2 meters vertically higher than the forward one.

(b) The vertical separation of the masthead lights of power-driven vessels shall be such that in all normal conditions of trim the after light will be seen over and separate from the forward light at a distance of 1000 meters from the stem when viewed from water level.

(c) The masthead light of a power-driven vessel of 12 meters but less than 20 meters in length shall be placed at a height above the gunwale of not less than 2.5 meters.

(d) The masthead light, or the all-round light described in rule 23(c), of a power-driven vessel of less than 12 meters in length shall be carried at least one meter higher than the sidelights.

(e) One of the two or three masthead lights prescribed for a power-driven vessel when engaged in towing or pushing another vessel shall be placed in the same position as either the forward masthead light or the after masthead light, pro-

2. *Vertical Positioning and Spacing of Lights*

(a) On a power-driven vessel of 20 metres or more in length the masthead lights shall be placed as follows:

(i) the forward masthead light, or if only one masthead light is carried, then that light, at a height above the hull of not less than 6 metres, and, if the breadth of the vessel exceeds 6 metres, then at a height above the hull not less than such breadth, so however that the light need not be placed at a greater height above the hull than 12 metres;

(ii) when two masthead lights are carried the after one shall be at least 4.5 metres vertically higher than the forward one.

(b) The vertical separation of masthead lights of power-driven vessels shall be such that in all normal conditions of trim the after light will be seen over and separate from the forward light at a distance of 1000 metres from the stem when viewed from sea level.

(c) The masthead light of a power-driven vessel of 12 metres but less than 20 metres in length shall be placed at a height above the gunwale of not less than 2.5 metres.

(d) A power-driven vessel of less than 12 metres in length may carry the uppermost light at a height of less than 2.5 metres above the gunwale. When however a masthead light is carried in addition to sidelights and a sternlight, then such masthead light shall be carried at least 1 metre higher than the sidelights.

(e) One of the two or three masthead lights prescribed for a power-driven vessel when en-

vided that the lowest after masthead light shall be at least 2 meters vertically higher than the highest forward masthead light.

(f)(1) The masthead light or lights prescribed in Rule 23(a) shall be so placed as to be above and clear of all other lights and obstructions except as described in paragraph (f)(2) of this section.

(2) When it is impracticable to carry the all-round lights prescribed in rule 27(b)(i) below the masthead lights, they may be carried above the after masthead light(s) or vertically in between the forward masthead light(s) and after masthead light(s), provided that in the latter case the requirement of § 84.05(d) shall be complied with.

(g) The sidelights of a power-driven vessel shall be placed at least one meter lower than the forward masthead light. They shall not be so low as to be interfered with by deck lights.

(h) [Reserved]

(i) When the Rules prescribe two or three lights to be carried in a vertical line, they shall be spaced as follows:

(1) On a vessel of 20 meters in length or more such lights shall be spaced not less than 1 meter apart, and the lowest of these lights shall, except where a towing light is required, be placed at a height of not less than 4 meters above the hull;

(2) On a vessel of less than 20 meters in length such lights shall be spaced not less than 1 meter apart and the lowest of these lights shall, except where a towing light is required, be placed at a height of not less than 2 meters above the hull;

(3) When three lights are carried they shall be equally spaced.

gaged in towing or pushing another vessel shall be placed in the same position as either the forward masthead light or the after masthead light; provided that, if carried on the aftermast, the lowest after masthead light shall be at least 4.5 metres vertically higher than the forward masthead light.

(f)—Same as Inland

(g) The sidelights of a power-driven vessel shall be placed at a height above the hull not greater than three quarters of that of the forward masthead light. They shall not be so low as to be interfered with by deck lights.

(h) The sidelights, if in a combined lantern and carried on a power-driven vessel of less than 20 metres in length, shall be placed not less than 1 metre below the masthead light.

(i) When the rules prescribe two or three lights to be carried in a vertical line, they shall be spaced as follows:

(i) on a vessel of 20 metres in length or more such lights shall be spaced not less than 2 metres apart, and the lowest of these lights shall, except where a towing light is required, be placed at a height of not less than 4 metres above the hull;

(ii) on a vessel of less than 20 metres in length such lights shall be spaced not less than 1 metre apart and the lowest of these lights shall, except where a towing light is required, be placed at a height of not less than 2 metres above the hull;

(iii) when three lights are carried they shall be equally spaced.

(j) The lower of the two all-round lights prescribed for a vessel when engaged in fishing shall be at a height above the sidelights not less than twice the distance between the two vertical lights.

INLAND

(j) The lower of the two all-round lights pre-scribed for a vessel when engaged in fishing shall be at a height above the sidelights not less than twice the distance between the two vertical lights.

(k) The forward anchor light prescribed in rule 30(a)(i), when two are carried, shall not be less than 4.5 meters above the after one. On a vessel of 50 meters or more in length this forward anchor light shall be placed at a height of not less than 6 meters above the hull.

§ 84.05 *Horizontal positioning and spacing of lights*

(a) Except as specified in paragraph (b) of this section, when two masthead lights are prescribed for a power-driven vessel, the horizontal distance between them shall not be less than one quarter of the length of the vessel but need not be more than 50 meters. The forward light shall be placed not more than one half of the length of the vessel from the stem.

(b) On power-driven vessels 50 meters but less than 60 meters in length operated on the Western Rivers, the horizontal distance between masthead lights shall not be less than 10 meters.

(c) On a power-driven vessel of 20 meters or more in length the sidelights shall not be placed in front of the forward masthead lights. They shall be placed at or near the side of the vessel.

(d) When the lights prescribed in rule 27(b)(i) are placed vertically between the forward mast-head light(s) and the after masthead light(s) these all-round lights shall be placed at a horizontal dis-tance of not less than 2 meters from the fore and aft centerline of the vessel in the athwartship direc-tion.

COLREGS

(k)—Same as Inland

3. *Horizontal Positioning and Spacing of Lights*

(a) When two masthead lights are prescribed for a power-driven vessel, the horizontal distance between them shall not be less than one half of the length of the vessel but need not be more than 100 metres. The forward light shall be placed not more than one quarter of the length of the vessel from the stem.

(b) On a power-driven vessel of 20 metres or more in length the sidelights shall not be placed in front of the forward masthead lights. They shall be placed at or near the side of the vessel.

(c) When the lights prescribed in Rule 27(b)(i) or Rule 28 are placed vertically between the for-ward masthead light(s) and the after masthead light(s) these all-round lights shall be placed at a horizontal distance of not less than 2 metres from the fore and aft centreline of the vessel in the athwartship direction.

§ 84.07 *Details of location of direction-indicating lights for fishing vessels, dredgers and vessels engaged in underwater operations*

(a) The light indicating the direction of the outlying gear from a vessel engaged in fishing as prescribed in rule 26(c)(ii) shall be placed at a horizontal distance of not less than 2 meters and not more than 6 meters away from the two all-round red and white lights. This light shall be placed not higher than the all-round white light prescribed in rule 26(c)(i) and not lower than the sidelights.

(b) The lights and shapes on a vessel engaged in dredging or underwater operations to indicate the obstructed side and/or the side on which it is safe to pass, as prescribed in rule 27(d)(i) and (ii), shall be placed at the maximum practical horizontal distance, but in no case less than 2 meters, from the lights or shapes prescribed in rule 27(b)(i) and (ii). In no case shall the upper of these lights or shapes be at a greater height than the lower of the three lights or shapes prescribed in rule 27(b)(i) and (ii).

§ 84.09 *Screens*

(a) The sidelights of vessels of 20 meters or more in length shall be fitted with mat black inboard screens and meet the requirements of § 84.17. On vessels of less than 20 meters in length, the sidelights, if necessary to meet the requirements of § 84.17, shall be fitted with mat black inboard screens. With a combined lantern, using a single vertical filament and a very narrow division between the green and red sections, external screens need not be fitted.

4. *Details of Location of Direction-Indicating Lights for Fishing Vessels, Dredgers and Vessels Engaged in Underwater Operations*

(a) The light indicating the direction of the outlying gear from a vessel engaged in fishing as prescribed in Rule 26(c)(ii) shall be placed at a horizontal distance of not less than 2 metres and not more than 6 metres away from the two all-round red and white lights. This light shall be placed not higher than the all-round white light prescribed in Rule 26(c)(i) and not lower than the sidelights.

(b) The lights and shapes on a vessel engaged in dredging or underwater operations to indicate the obstructed side and/or the side on which it is safe to pass, as prescribed in Rule 27(d)(i) and (ii), shall be placed at the maximum practical horizontal distance, but in no case less than 2 metres, from the lights or shapes prescribed in Rule 27(b)(i) and (ii). In no case shall the upper of these lights or shapes be at a greater height than the lower of the three lights or shapes prescribed in Rule 27(b)(i) and (ii).

5. *Screens for Sidelights*

The sidelights of vessels of 20 metres or more in length shall be fitted with inboard screens painted matt black, and meeting the requirements of Section 9 of this Annex. On vessels of less than 20 metres in length the sidelights, if necessary to meet the requirements of Section 9 of this Annex, shall be fitted with inboard matt black screens. With a combined lantern, using a single vertical filament and a very narrow division between the green and red sections, external screens need not be fitted.

(b) On power-driven vessels less than 12 meters in length constructed after July 31, 1983, the masthead light, or the all-round light described in rule 23(c) shall be screened to prevent direct illumination of the vessel forward of the operator's position.

§ 84.11 *Shapes*

(a) Shapes shall be black and of the following sizes:

(1) A ball shall have a diameter of not less than 0.6 meter;

(2) A cone shall have a base diameter of not less than 0.6 meter and a height equal to its diameter;

(3) A diamond shape shall consist of two cones (as defined in paragraph (a)(2) of this section) having a common base.

(b) The vertical distance between shapes shall be at least 1.5 meter.

(c) In a vessel of less than 20 meters in length shapes of lesser dimensions but commensurate with the size of the vessel may be used and the distance apart may be correspondingly reduced.

§ 84.13 *Color specification of lights*

(a) The chromaticity of all navigation lights shall conform to the following standards, which lie within the boundaries of the area of the diagram specified for each color by the International Commission on Illumination (CIE), in the "Colors of

6. *Shapes*

(a) Shapes shall be black and of the following sizes:

(i) a ball shall have a diameter of not less than 0.6 metre;

(ii) a cone shall have a base diameter of not less than 0.6 metre and a height equal to its diameter;

(iii) a cylinder shall have a diameter of at least 0.6 metre and a height of twice its diameter;

(iv) a diamond shape shall consist of two cones as defined in (ii) above having a common base.

(b) The vertical distance between shapes shall be at least 1.5 metre.

(c) In a vessel of less than 20 metres in length shapes of lesser dimensions but commensurate with the size of the vessel may be used and the distance apart may be correspondingly reduced.

7. *Colour Specification of Lights*

The chromaticity of all navigation lights shall conform to the following standards, which lie within the boundaries of the area of the diagram specified for each colour by the International Commission on Illumination (CIE).

Light Signals", which is incorporated by reference. It is Publication CIE No. 2.2. (TC–1.6), 1975, and is available from the Illumination Engineering Society, 345 East 47th Street, New York, NY 10017. It is also available for inspection at the Office of the Federal Register, Room 8401, 1100 L Street N.W., Washington, DC 20408. This incorporation by reference was approved by the Director of the Federal Register.

(b) The boundaries of the area for each color are given by indicating the corner co-ordinates, which are as follows:

(1) *White:*

| x | 0.525 | 0.525 | 0.452 | 0.310 | 0.310 | 0.443 |
| y | 0.382 | 0.440 | 0.440 | 0.348 | 0.283 | 0.382 |

(2) *Green:*

| x | 0.028 | 0.009 | 0.300 | 0.203 |
| y | 0.385 | 0.723 | 0.511 | 0.356 |

(3) *Red:*

| x | 0.680 | 0.660 | 0.735 | 0.721 |
| y | 0.320 | 0.320 | 0.265 | 0.259 |

(4) *Yellow:*

| x | 0.612 | 0.618 | 0.575 | 0.575 |
| y | 0.382 | 0.382 | 0.425 | 0.406 |

§ 84.15 *Intensity of lights*

(a) The minimum luminous intensity of lights shall be calculated by using the formula:
$$I = 3.43 \times 10^6 \times T \times D^2 \times K^{-D}$$
where I is luminous intensity in candelas under service conditions.
T is threshold factor 2×10^{-7} lux,
  D is range of visibility (luminous range) of the light in nautical miles,

The boundaries of the area for each colour are given by indicating the corner co-ordinates, which are as follows:

(i) *White:*

| x | 0.525 | 0.525 | 0.452 | 0.310 | 0.310 | 0.443 |
| y | 0.382 | 0.440 | 0.440 | 0.348 | 0.283 | 0.382 |

(ii) *Green:*

| x | 0.028 | 0.009 | 0.300 | 0.203 |
| y | 0.385 | 0.723 | 0.511 | 0.356 |

(iii) *Red:*

| x | 0.680 | 0.660 | 0.735 | 0.721 |
| y | 0.320 | 0.320 | 0.265 | 0.259 |

(iv) *Yellow:*

| x | 0.612 | 0.618 | 0.575 | 0.575 |
| y | 0.382 | 0.382 | 0.425 | 0.406 |

8. *Intensity of Lights*

(a) The minimum luminous intensity of lights shall be calculated by using the formula:
$$I = 3.43 \times 10^6 \times T \times D^2 \times K^{-D}$$
where I   is luminous intensity in candelas under service conditions,
  T   is threshold factor 2×10^{-7} lux,
  D   is range of visibility (luminous range) of the light in nautical miles,

INLAND

K is atmospheric transmissivity. For prescribed lights the value of K shall be 0.8, corresponding to a meteorological visibility of approximately 13 nautical miles.

(b) A selection of figures derived from the formula is given in Table 84.15(b)

Table 84.15(b)

Range of visibility (luminous range) of light in nautical miles D	Minimum luminous intensity of light in candelas for K = 0.8
1	0.9
2	4.3
3	12
4	27
5	52
6	94

§ 84.17 *Horizontal sectors*

(a)(1) In the forward direction, sidelights as fitted on the vessel shall show the minimum required intensities. The intensities shall decrease to reach practical cut-off between 1 and 3 degrees outside the prescribed sectors.

(2) For sternlights and masthead lights and at 22.5 degrees abaft the beam for sidelights, the minimum required intensities shall be maintained over the arc of the horizon up to 5 degrees within the limits of the sectors prescribed in rule 21. From 5 degrees within the prescribed sectors the intensity may decrease by 50 percent up to the

COLREGS

K is atmospheric transmissivity. For prescribed lights the value of K shall be 0.8, corresponding to a meteorological visibility of approximately 13 nautical miles.

(b) A selection of figures derived from the formula is given in the following table:

Range of visibility (luminous range) of light in nautical miles D	Luminous intensity of light in candelas for K = 0.8 I
1	0.9
2	4.3
3	12.0
4	27.0
5	52.0
6	94.0

Note: The maximum luminous intensity of navigation lights should be limited to avoid undue glare. This shall not be achieved by a variable control of the luminous intensity.

9. *Horizontal Sectors*

(a)—Same as Inland

prescribed limits; it shall decrease steadily to reach practical cut-off at not more than 5 degrees outside the prescribed sectors.

(b) All-round lights shall be so located as not to be obscured by masts, topmasts or structures within angular sectors of more than 6 degrees, except anchor lights prescribed in rule 30, which need not be placed at an impracticable height above the hull, and the all-round white light described in rule 23(d), which may not be obscured at all.

§ 84.19 *Vertical sectors*

(a) The vertical sectors of electric lights as fitted, with the exception of lights on sailing vessels and on unmanned barges, shall ensure that:

(1) At least the required minimum intensity is maintained at all angles from 5 degrees above to 5 degrees below the horizontal;
(2) At least 60 percent of the required minimum intensity is maintained from 7.5 degrees above to 7.5 degrees below the horizontal.

(b) In the case of sailing vessels the vertical sectors of electric lights as fitted shall ensure that:

(1) At least the required minimum intensity is maintained at all angles from 5 degrees above to 5 degrees below the horizontal;
(2) At least 50 percent of the required minimum intensity is maintained from 25 degrees above to 25 degrees below the horizontal.

(c) In the case of unmanned barges the minimum required intensity of electric lights as fitted shall be maintained on the horizontal.

(b) All-round lights shall be so located as not to be obscured by masts, topmasts or structures within angular sectors of more than 6 degrees, except anchor lights prescribed in Rule 30, which need not be placed at an impracticable height above the hull.

10. *Vertical Sectors*

(a) The vertical sectors of electric lights as fitted, with the exception of lights on sailing vessels shall ensure that:

(i) at least the required minimum intensity is maintained at all angles from 5 degrees above to 5 degrees below the horizontal;
(ii) at least 60 percent of the required minimum intensity is maintained from 7.5 degrees above to 7.5 degrees below the horizontal.

(b)—Same as Inland

(c) In the case of lights other than electric these specifications shall be met as closely as possible.

(d) In the case of lights other than electric lights these specifications shall be met as closely as possible.

§ 84.21 *Intensity of non-electric lights*

Non-electric lights shall so far as practicable comply with the minimum intensities, as specified in the Table given in § 84.15.

§ 84.23 *Maneuvering light*

Notwithstanding the provisions of § 84.03(f), the maneuvering light described in rule 34(b) shall be placed approximately in the same fore and aft vertical plane as the masthead light or lights and, where practicable, at a minimum height of one-half meter vertically above the forward masthead light, provided that it shall be carried not less than one-half meter vertically above or below the after masthead light. On a vessel where only one masthead light is carried the maneuvering light, if fitted, shall be carried where it can best be seen, not less than one-half meter vertically apart from the masthead light.

§ 84.25 *Approval.* [*Reserved*]

11. *Intensity of Non-Electric Lights*

Nonelectric lights shall so far as practicable comply with the minimum intensities, as specified in the Table given in Section 8 of this Annex.

12. *Manoeuvring Light*

Notwithstanding the provisions of paragraph 2(f) of this Annex the manoeuvring light described in Rule 34(b) shall be placed in the same fore and aft vertical plane as the masthead light or lights and, where practicable, at a minimum height of 2 metres vertically above the forward masthead light, provided that it shall be carried not less than 2 metres vertically above or below the after masthead light. On a vessel where only one masthead light is carried the manoeuvring light, if fitted, shall be carried where it can best be seen, not less than 2 metres vertically apart from the masthead light.

13. *Approval*

The construction of lights and shapes and the installation of lights on board the vessel shall be to the satisfaction of the appropriate authority of the State whose flag the vessel is entitled to fly.

ANNEX II

ADDITIONAL SIGNALS FOR FISHING VESSELS FISHING IN CLOSE PROXIMITY

ANNEX II

ADDITIONAL SIGNALS FOR FISHING VESSELS FISHING IN CLOSE PROXIMITY

1. *General*

The lights mentioned herein shall, if exhibited in pursuance of Rule 26(d), be placed where they can best be seen. They shall be at least 0.9 meter apart but at a lower level than lights prescribed in Rule 26(b)(i) and (c)(i) contained in the Navigational Rules Act of 1980. The lights shall be visible all around the horizon at a distance of at least 1 mile but at a lesser distance from the lights prescribed by these Rules for fishing vessels.

2. *Signals for Trawlers*

(a) Vessels when engaged in trawling, whether using demersal or pelagic gear, may exhibit:

(i) when shooting their nets: two white lights in a vertical line;
(ii) when hauling their nets: one white light over one red light in a vertical line;
(iii) when the net has come fast upon an obstruction: two red lights in a vertical line.

(b) Each vessel engaged in pair trawling may exhibit:

(i) by night, a searchlight directed forward and in the direction of the other vessel of the pair;

Annex II to the COLREGS is identical to Annex II of the Inland Rules.

(ii) when shooting or hauling their nets or when their nets have come fast upon an obstruction, the lights prescribed in paragraph (a) above.

3. *Signals for Purse Seiners*

Vessels engaged in fishing with purse seine gear may exhibit two yellow lights in a vertical line. These lights shall flash alternately every second and with equal light and occultation duration. These lights may be exhibited only when the vessel is hampered by its fishing gear.

ANNEX III

TECHNICAL DETAILS OF
SOUND SIGNAL APPLIANCES

Subpart A—Whistles

§86.01 *Frequencies and range of audibility*

The fundamental frequency of the signal shall lie within the range 70–525 Hz. The range of audibility of the signal from a whistle shall be determined by those frequencies, which may include the fundamental and/or one or more higher frequencies, which lie within the frequency ranges and provide the sound pressure levels specified in § 86.05.

ANNEX III

TECHNICAL DETAILS OF
SOUND SIGNAL APPLIANCES

1. *Whistles*
   (a) *Frequencies and range of audibility.* The fundamental frequency of the signal shall lie within the range 70-700 Hz.
   The range of audibility of the signal from a whistle shall be determined by those frequencies, which may include the fundamental and/or one or more higher frequencies, which lie within the range 180-700 Hz ($\pm$ 1 percent) and which provide the sound pressure levels specified in paragraph 1(c) below.

§ 86.03 *Limits of fundamental frequencies*

To ensure a wide variety of whistle characteristics, the fundamental frequency of a whistle shall be between the following limits:

(a) 70–200 Hz, for a vessel 200 meters or more in length;

(b) 130–350 Hz, for a vessel 75 meters but less than 200 meters in length;

(c) 250–525 Hz, for a vessel less than 75 meters in length.

§ 86.05 *Sound signal intensity and range of audibility*

A whistle on a vessel shall provide, in the direction of the forward axis of the whistle and at a distance of 1 meter from it, a sound pressure level in at least one ⅓-octave band of not less than the appropriate figure given in Table 86.05 within the following frequency ranges (±1 percent):

(a) 130–1200 Hz, for a vessel 75 meters or more in length;

(b) 250–1600 Hz, for a vessel 20 meters but less than 75 meters in length;

(c) 250–2100 Hz, for a vessel 12 meters but less than 20 meters in length.

In practice the range at which a whistle may be heard is extremely variable and depends critically on weather conditions; the values given can be regarded as typical but under conditions of strong wind or high ambient noise level at the listening post the range may be much reduced.

(b) *Limits of fundamental frequencies.* To ensure a wide variety of whistle characteristics, the fundamental frequency of a whistle shall be between the following limits:

(i) 70-200 Hz, for a vessel 200 metres or more in length;

(ii) 130-350 Hz, for a vessel 75 metres but less than 200 metres in length;

(iii) 250-700 Hz, for a vessel less than 75 metres in length.

(c) *Sound signal intensity and range of audibility.* A whistle fitted in a vessel shall provide, in the direction of maximum intensity of the whistle and at a distance of 1 metre from it, a sound pressure level in at least one 1/3-octave band within the range of frequencies 180-700 Hz (± 1 percent) of not less than the appropriate figure given in the table below.

Length of vessel in metres	1/3d-octave band level at 1 metre in dB referred to 2×10^{-5} N/m^2	Audibility range in nautical miles
200 or more	143	2
75 but less than 200....	138	1.5
20 but less than 75.....	130	1
Less than 20	120	0.5

The range of audibility in the table above is for information and is approximately the range at

Table 86.05

Length of vessel in meters	Fundamental frequency range (Hz)	For measured frequencies (Hz)	⅓-octave band level at 1 meter in dB referred to $2 \times 10^{-5} N/m^2$	Audibility range in nautical miles
200 or more	70–200	130–180	145	2
		180–250	143	
		250-1200	140	
75 but less than 200	130–350	130–180	140	1.5
		180–250	138	
		250–1200	134	
20 but less than 75	250–525	250–450	130	1.0
		450–800	125	
		800–1600	121	
12 but less than 20	250–525	250–450	120	0.5
		450–800	115	
		800–2100	111	

NOTE.—The range of audibility in the table above is for information and is approximately the range at which a whistle may usually be heard on its forward axis in conditions of still air on board a vessel having average background noise level at the listening posts (taken to be 68 dB in the octave band centered on 250 Hz and 63 dB in the octave band centered on 500 Hz).

which a whistle may be heard on its forward axis with 90 percent probability in conditions of still air on board a vessel having average background noise level at the listening posts (taken to be 68 dB in the octave band centred on 250 Hz and 63 dB in the octave band centred on 500 Hz).

In practice the range at which a whistle may be heard is extremely variable and depends critically on weather conditions; the values given can be regarded as typical but under conditions of strong wind or high ambient noise level at the listening post the range may be much reduced.

§ 86.07 *Directional properties*

The sound pressure level of a directional whistle shall be not more than 4 dB below the sound pressure level specified in § 86.05 in any direction in the horizontal plane within ±45 degrees of the forward axis. The sound pressure level of the whistle in any other direction in the horizontal plane shall not be more than 10 dB less than the sound pressure level specified for the forward axis, so that the range of audibility in any direction will be at least half the range required on the forward axis. The sound pressure level shall be measured in that one-third octave band which determines the audibility range.

(d) *Directional properties.* The sound pressure level of a directional whistle shall be not more than 4 dB below the prescribed sound pressure level on the axis at any direction in the horizontal plane within ±45 degrees of the axis. The sound pressure level at any other direction in the horizontal plane shall be not more than 10 dB below the prescribed sound pressure level on the axis, so that the range in any direction will be at least half the range on the forward axis. The sound pressure level shall be measured in that one-third octave band which determines the audibility range.

§ 86.09 *Positioning of whistles*

(a) When a directional whistle is to be used as the only whistle on the vessel and is permanently installed, it shall be installed with its forward axis directed forward.

(b) A whistle shall be placed as high as practicable on a vessel, in order to reduce interception of

(e) *Positioning of whistles.* When a directional whistle is to be used as the only whistle on a vessel, it shall be installed with its maximum intensity directed straight ahead.

A whistle shall be placed as high as practicable on a vessel, in order to reduce interception of the emitted sound by obstructions and also to mini-

the emitted sound by obstructions and also to minimize hearing damage risk to personnel. The sound pressure level of the vessel's own signal at listening posts shall not exceed 110 dB(A) and so far as practicable should not exceed 100 dB(A).

§ 86.11 *Fitting of more than one whistle*

If whistles are fitted at a distance apart of more than 100 meters, they shall not be sounded simultaneously.

Note.—If due to the presence of obstructions the sound field of a single whistle or of one of the whistles referred to in § 86.11 is likely to have a zone of greatly reduced signal level, a combined whistle system should be fitted so as to overcome this reduction.

§86.13 *Combined whistle systems*

(a) A combined whistle system is a number of whistles (sound emitting sources) operated together. For the purposes of the Rules a combined whistle system is to be regarded as a single whistle.

(b) The whistles of a combined system shall—

(1) Be located at a distance apart of not more than 100 meters.

(2) Be sounded simultaneously.

(3) Each have a fundamental frequency different from those of the others by at least 10 Hz, and

mize hearing damage risk to personnel. The sound pressure level of the vessel's own signal at listening posts shall not exceed 110 dB (A) and so far as practicable should not exceed 100 dB (A).

(f) *Fitting of more than one whistle.* If whistles are fitted at a distance apart of more than 100 metres, it shall be so arranged that they are not sounded simultaneously.

(g) *Combined whistle systems.* If due to the presence of obstructions the sound field of a single whistle or of one of the whistles referred to in paragraph 1(f) above is likely to have a zone of greatly reduced signal level, it is recommended that a combined whistle system be fitted so as to overcome this reduction. For the purposes of the rules a combined whistle system is to be regarded as a single whistle. The whistles of a combined system shall be located at a distance apart of not more than 100 metres and arranged to be sounded simultaneously. The frequency of any one whistle shall differ from those of the others by at least 10 Hz.

(4) Have a tonal characteristic appropriate for the length of vessel which shall be evidenced by at least two-thirds of the whistles in the combined system having fundamental frequencies falling within the limits prescribed in § 86.03, or if there are only two whistles in the combined system, by the higher fundamental frequency falling within the limits prescribed in § 86.03.

§ 86.15 *Towing vessel whistles*

A power-driven vessel normally engaged in pushing ahead or towing alongside may, at all times, use a whistle whose characteristic falls within the limits prescribed by § 86.03 for the longest customary composite length of the vessel and its tow.

Subpart B—Bell or Gong

§ 86.21 *Intensity of signal*

A bell or gong, or other device having similar sound characteristics shall produce a sound pressure level of not less than 110 dB at 1 meter.

§ 86.23 *Construction*

Bells and gongs shall be made of corrosion-resistant material and designed to give a clear tone. The diameter of the mouth of the bell shall be not less than 300 mm for vessels of more than 20 meters in length, and shall be not less than 200 mm for vessels of 12 to 20 meters in length. The mass of the striker shall be not less than 3 percent of the mass of the bell. The striker shall be capable of manual operation. Note: When practicable, a power-driven bell striker is recommended to ensure constant force.

2. *Bell or Gong*

(a) *Intensity of signal.* A bell or gong, or other device having similar sound characteristics shall produce a sound pressure level of not less than 110 dB at a distance of 1 metre from it.

(b) *Construction.* Bells and gongs shall be made of corrosion-resistant material and designed to give a clear tone. The diameter of the mouth of the bell shall be not less than 300 mm for vessels 20 metres or more in length, and shall be not less than 200 mm for vessels of 12 metres or more but of less than 20 metres in length. Where practicable, a power-driven bell striker is recommended to ensure constant force but manual operation shall be possible. The mass of the striker shall be not less than 3 percent of the mass of the bell.

INLAND

Subpart C—Approval

§ 86.31 *Approval* [*Reserved*]

ANNEX IV

DISTRESS SIGNALS

The draft (proposed) for Annex IV to the Inland Rules is identical to Annex IV of the COLREGS, but provisions pertaining to strobe lights may be added.

COLREGS

3. *Approval*

The construction of sound signal appliances, their performance and their installation on board the vessel shall be to the satisfaction of the appropriate authority of the State whose flag the vessel is entitled to fly.

ANNEX IV

DISTRESS SIGNALS

1. The following signals, used or exhibited either together or separately, indicate distress and need of assistance:

(a) a gun or other explosive signal fired at intervals of about a minute;

(b) a continuous sounding with any fog-signalling apparatus;

(c) rockets or shells, throwing red stars fired one at a time at short intervals;

(d) a signal made by radiotelegraphy or by any other signalling method consisting of the group . . . — — — . . . (SOS) in the Morse Code;

(e) a signal sent by radiotelephony consisting of the spoken word "Mayday";

(f) the International Code Signal of distress indicated by N.C.;

(g) a signal consisting of a square flag having above or below it a ball or anything resembling a ball;

(h) flames on the vessel (as from a burning tar barrel, oil barrel, etc.);

(i) a rocket parachute flare or a hand flare showing a red light;

(j) a smoke signal giving off orange-coloured smoke;

(k) slowly and repeatedly raising and lowering arms outstretched to each side;

(l) the radiotelegraph alarm signal;

(m) the radiotelephone alarm signal;

(n) signals transmitted by emergency position-indicating radio beacons.

2. The use or exhibition of any of the foregoing signals except for the purpose of indicating distress and need of assistance and the use of other signals which may be confused with any of the above signals is prohibited.

3. Attention is drawn to the relevant sections of the International Code of Signals, the Merchant Ship Search and Rescue Manual and the following signals:

(a) a piece of orange-coloured canvas with either a black square and circle or other appropriate symbol (for identification from the air);

(b) a dye marker.

D Selected Court Cases

ATLANTIC MUTUAL INSURANCE CO. v. ABC INSURANCE CO. 645 F. 2d 528 (1981)

Protection and indemnity insurer of supply vessel and her owner brought subrogation action against owner and insurer of towing vessel with which it collided for contribution to $58,544 it expended in settlement of personal injury claim arising out of the collision. The United States District Court for the Eastern District of Louisiana, at New Orleans, Robert F. Collins, J., denied recovery and plaintiff appealed. The Court of Appeals, Brown, Circuit Judge, held that district court's total exoneration of towing vessel was clearly erroneous, since towing vessel failed to overcome its burden of showing by all reasonable probabilities that her two violations of rules of the road, in failing to blow its fog signals although situation clearly called for it and instead sounding passing signal at time when supply vessel was not in view, did not contribute to cause of the collision.

Reversed and remanded.

. . .

Before BROWN, POLITZ and TATE, Circuit Judges.

JOHN R. BROWN, Circuit Judge:

This law suit concerns a collision between two vessels, M/V KIMMIE C and M/V CHARLEEN B, heading in opposite directions in fog in the Eugene Island Channel of the Atchafalaya Bay. Appellant, protection and indemnity insurer of CHARLEEN B, brought this subrogation action for contribution to the $58,544.00 it expended in settlement of a personal injury claim arising out of the collision. The District Court denied recovery, finding that the negligence of CHARLEEN B was the sole proximate cause of the collision. Because we find the District Court's total exoneration of KIMMIE C to be clearly erroneous, we reverse and remand.

On January 12, 1976, KIMMIE C, a towing vessel 61 feet long and 19 feet wide, left Morgan City, Louisiana pushing a flat-deck barge 140 feet long and 40 feet wide loaded with drilling equipment. KIMMIE C was proceeding south through the Eugene Island Channel, a dredged channel not less than 200 feet wide and 10 feet deep, on her way into the Gulf of Mexico. At the same time CHARLEEN B, a supply vessel 91 feet long and 24 feet wide, was proceeding north through the channel towards Morgan City.

Both vessels encountered dense fog with visibility limited to 50 to 150 feet. At a point when the two vessels were approximately a mile and a half apart, the captain of each vessel spotted the other vessel on radar but each was unsuccessful in making radio contact with the other. Radar was of little or no use when the vessels were within one quarter mile of each other. The District Court found that in spite of the dense fog, neither vessel blew fog signals. The Court further found that KIMMIE C proceeded at a moderate speed and kept to the starboard (west) side of the channel. The captain of CHARLEEN B, on the other hand, so the Court found, negligently failed to keep his vessel to the starboard (east) side of the channel so as to permit a port-to-port passing.* The Court determined that the vessels collided in the western half of the Channel as the sole result of the negligence of CHARLEEN B.

Roy Bellamy, a cook on CHARLEEN B, was allegedly injured during the collision. The Atlantic Mutual Insurance Company ("Atlantic"), protection and indemnity insurer of CHARLEEN B and her owner, settled Bellamy's personal injury claims for $58,544.00. Atlantic instituted this sub-

rogation action for contribution against the owner, Garber Brothers, Inc., and insurer, ABC Insurance Company, of KIMMIE C. Because the Court found that the negligence of KIMMIE C was not a contributing cause of the collision, Atlantic was denied recovery.

[1] Atlantic assigns a number of points of error on this appeal. . . .

We do not reach Atlantic's various points of error as to the District Court's findings of fact. We believe that on the basis of those findings and the uncontroverted testimony of the captain of KIMMIE C the Court's determination of no contribution on the part of KIMMIE C is clearly wrong.

On the day of collision, KIMMIE C committed at least two violations of the rules of the road. First, as the District Court explicitly found, KIMMIE C failed to blow its fog signals although the situation clearly called for it. Second, as the captain of KIMMIE C unequivocally testified, KIMMIE C instead sounded a passing signal at a time when CHARLEEN B was not in view.†

---

*The Court found that a current, moving at approximately four miles per hour, crosses the Channel from northeast to southeast, and that the captain of CHARLEEN B was aware of this current.

† . . . The following is an exchange between the captain of the KIMMIE C and counsel for Atlantic:

Q When you were a quarter of a mile apart, as I understand your earlier testimony, you said you heard a whistle. Is that true?

A That is true.

Q And you answered this whistle signal with a passing signal, one short and distinct blast. Is that true?

A Yes, that is true.

Q What does the whistle signal of one short and distinct blast mean?

A It means you are going to pass on the one-whistle side. In other words, you are supposed to maintain your side. He was supposed to be on the east side and I was supposed to be on the west side. That is the passing signal.

Q At this time you were not in sight of one another. Is that correct?

[2] The Rule of *The Pennsylvania* enjoys continued validity in collision cases.‡ That Rule provides that when a ship violates a statutory rule intended to prevent collision, "the burden rests upon the ship of showing not merely that her fault might not have been one of the causes, or that it probably was not, but that it could not have been. Such a rule is necessary to enforce obedience to the mandate of the statute.". . .

[3] We find that on the facts of this case KIMMIE C clearly failed to overcome its burden of showing that "by all reasonable probabilities" her violations of the rules of the road did not contribute to the cause of the collision. Although the

---

A That is correct.

Q He was approximately a quarter of a mile away, as best you can tell, from your radar?

A Right.

Q Do you realize, Captain, under the Rules of the Road, the Rules of the Road for inland waters, it was wrong to sound passing signals when not in sight of another vessel?

A I realized it after I did it, but he blew one whistle and I answered him with one.

Q Did you hear that whistle signal,—the whistle signal you heard, did it seem to come from forward of your beam, coming from ahead of you?

A That's right.

Q But it was still foggy and you could not see him?

A It was.

Q Isn't it true, Captain, that at this point in time you should have kept blowing your fog signal?

A I should have, yes.

Q And you were wrong not to do so?

A I was.

‡*The Pennsylvania* Rule was in no way affected by *United States v. Reliable Transfer Co.*, 421 U.S. 397, 95 S.Ct. 1708, 44 L.Ed.2d 251 (1975) which overruled *The Pennsylvania* only to the extent of abolishing the mutual fault-equal contribution rule and substituting the new rule of allocation determined by the degree of comparative fault. *See, Tug Ocean Prince, Inc. v. United States*, 584 F.2d 1151, 1160 (2d Cir. 1978).

District Court might find that "but for" CHARLEEN B being on the wrong side of the Channel, the collision would not have occurred, it is also reasonably probable that if KIMMIE C had not sounded a passing signal, and instead had sounded a fog signal, at a time when the view from the wheel house barely extended past the bow of the barge she was pushing,§ the vessels would not have proceeded to pass and thus would not have collided. This fault on the part of KIMMIE C cannot be dismissed as "merely fault in the abstract.". . .

While we determine the District Court's finding of no fault on the part of KIMMIE C to be clearly erroneous, we do not pass on what measure of damages, if any, is appropriate in this case. First, we leave the question of allocation to be determined by the District Court in a manner consistent with *United States v. Reliable Transfer Co., Inc.*, 421 U.S. 397, 95 S.Ct. 1708, 44 L.Ed.2d 251 (1975), and this opinion. Second, we leave for the District Court the question of the validity of the personal injury claim of Bellamy and the reasonableness of the settlement of that claim.

REVERSED and REMANDED.

COMPLAINT OF PACIFIC BULK CARRIERS, INC.
639 F.2d 72 (1980)

In action arising from collision of two ships, the United States District Court for the Southern District of New York, Charles E. Stewart, J., 493 F.Supp. 192, found burdened vessel eighty percent

§As discussed previously, the District Court found that at the time of the collision, visibility was limited to 50 to 150 feet. The barge which was being pushed by KIMMIE C was itself 140 feet long.

libel and privileged vessel twenty percent libel for collision, and privileged vessel appealed. The Court of Appeals, Moore, Circuit Judge, held that: (1) burdened ship travelling southwesterly in a crossing situation under International Rules was negligent and at fault with respect to collision with privileged ship traveling southeasterly where she failed to keep an adequate lookout, failed to sound two blasts when turning to port, and failed to use her radar, her master was below and not on bridge although he knew they were navigating in a heavily traveled area, and ship went hard to port immediately before collision when a turn hard to starboard might have avoided collision, and (2) privileged vessel could not be faulted to extent of 20% with respect to collision notwithstanding decision of her master to set an eastbound course across westbound traffic lane of the traffic separation scheme where the scheme had not been approved by the Intergovernmental Maritime Consultative Organization and had not attained the status of a custom.

Affirmed as modified.

. . .

Before MOORE, FRIENDLY and MESS-KILL, Circuit Judges.

MOORE, Circuit Judge:

This litigation arises from the collision of two ships, the M.V. Atlantic Hope (Hope) and the S.S. American Aquarius (Aquarius), in international waters south of Japan early in the morning of April 20, 1973. The trial court (Honorable Charles E. Stewart, Judge, Southern District of New York), based on findings of fact, held Pacific Bulk Carriers, Inc., as owner of the Hope, 80%

liable for the collision and United States Lines, Inc., as owner of the Aquarius, 20% liable. Yamashita Shinnihon Kisen, K.K., as owner of the M.V. Sadoharu Maru (Maru), another ship which had crossed between the ships before they collided, was held not liable. Hope and Aquarius both appeal from the judgment below.

The only issue before the trial court was the responsibility of the parties for the damages resulting from the collision, all other claims having been settled. On appeal the primary issue is the trial court's apportionment of fault: 80% attributable to the Hope; 20% to the Aquarius. From the facts as found by the trial court we believe that the Hope is 100% liable and that the Aquarius should be exonerated. To this extent we modify the decision below.

The lower court has adequately outlined the facts in its opinion, 493 F.Supp. 192, and we sketch only an outline of the events which occurred in the early morning hours on April 20, 1973. At approximately 3:20 a.m. the weather was dark and overcast with light rain, but visibility was good at six–eight miles. Two ships, the Hope and Maru, were headed in a southwesterly direction. Aquarius was traveling in a southeasterly direction so as to cross in front of Hope and Maru. Before the collision, Maru had passed Hope to Maru's starboard, then turned to starboard some ¾ mile ahead of Hope to cross between Hope and Aquarius. As the privileged ship (to Hope's starboard) in a crossing situation under the International Rules . . . , Aquarius kept its speed up until immediately before the collision. Hope, the burdened ship . . . was required to keep out of Aquarius' way, but it also kept up its speed. Hope turned hard to port immediately before the collision, and struck Aquarius aft on the port side. The court found that a turn hard to starboard at the last moment would have avoided the collision.

We affirm the judgment of the district court insofar as it exonerates the Maru and holds Hope liable. The trial court found that the Maru was some ¾ mile in front of Hope when it crossed between the two ships, and that "when Maru turned to cross Hope, she was past and clear and there was no danger of collision". . . . She was properly exonerated.

[1] The evidence of Hope's negligence was overwhelming. She failed to keep an adequate lookout as required . . .; she failed to sound two blasts when turning to port . . .; she failed to use her radar; the Master was below and not on the bridge although he knew they were navigating in a heavily traveled area; and the ship went hard to port immediately before the collision, when a turn hard to starboard might have avoided the collision. We agree with the other findings of fact set out in the district court opinion which bespeak Hope's fault in this collision. . . .

The question of Aquarius' liability arises out of the effect, if any, to be given to a traffic separation scheme (TSS) designed by the Japan Captain's Association, a non-governmental, unofficial body. In this area of heavy ocean traffic, the scheme provides separate lanes for traffic in opposite directions, the lanes being separated by a buffer zone. Each lane is one-and-a-half miles wide and the buffer zone one mile wide. The TSS involved in this case, known as the Shiono Misaki, as found by the court, had not been submitted to, or approved by, the Intergovernmental Maritime Consultative Organization (IMCO), "the only organization empowered to recommend traffic separation lanes in international waters". . . .

[2] The district court found that: "As to the Aquarius, she clearly was proceeding in the wrong direction in the westbound lane of the Shiono Misaki TSS". . . . This fact, however, is not determinative of Aquarius' liability because Aquarius and Hope had sighted each other at some distance. Visibility was six–eight miles and regardless of any TSS "it is clear that the applicable International Rules controlled once Aquarius had sighted Hope and Maru.". . . Under these rules, Aquarius was the privileged vessel and it was the duty of the Hope to keep out of her way and to take whatever affirmative action was necessary to do so. This the Hope failed to do.

In assessing 20% liability against the Aquarius, the trial court relied greatly on a recent English admiralty case, *The Genimar*, [1977] 2 Lloyd's Rep. 17. The factual situation there was somewhat different. Unlike the setting in *The Genimar*, the TSS in this case was not marked on the official government navigation charts for the area. Three of the four ships in the area of this collision were not complying with the lanes. Hope knew she was the burdened ship here, and had at least six miles of open water with good visibility in which to maneuver. Under these circumstances had the Hope followed the applicable International Rules, the collision could have been avoided.

[3, 4] Defining good seamanship as requiring "compliance by the vessel with a collision-preventing scheme of which her master ha[s] full knowledge" . . . the trial court faulted the Aquarius to the extent of 20% for the decision of

its master to set an eastbound course across the westbound traffic lane of the TSS. With this definition and the consequent finding of poor seamanship we do not agree. As noted above, the traffic separation scheme in question had not been approved by IMCO. Granting that some sailing rules not having official status can achieve the force of law by custom or usage, the trial court found—correctly, in our view—that the Shiono Misaki TSS had not attained the status of a custom. We decline further to extend the net of liability. Mere knowledge of the existence of a traffic separation scheme lacking the force of law does not create an enforceable duty to observe it. Thus, the action of the Aquarius in our opinion cannot be fairly characterized as a failure to conform with good seamanship.

[5] However, even if we were to find that the Aquarius was bound to follow the TSS, our disposition of this appeal would not be altered. The vessels were in international waters. The Aquarius was entitled to proceed in accordance with, and to rely on, the standard rules applicable to international waters. The Hope had at least six miles of open water in which to maneuver so as to avoid the Aquarius. The vessels remained within sight of each other during this distance. Each vessel knew of the presence of the other and its maritime obligations. Under these circumstances the TSS, even if elevated in status, would not supersede [the] applicable Rule. . . . The fact that the Aquarius was in the "wrong" lane according to the TSS did not justify the Hope in disregarding international rules. The collision was caused by such disregard and any fault attributable to the Aquarius was not a factor.

Even in *The Genimar* the court said: "There may well be cases of collisions in clear weather, where contravention of a traffic separation scheme by one of the colliding ships, though a fault, will nevertheless not be a causative fault. A typical case of that kind would be where, although the area is usually busy, no ships other than the colliding ships are about at the time, and they see one another clearly at a distance of several miles", [1977] 2 Lloyd's Rep. at 26. Although in this case there were other vessels in the vicinity the trial court found they did not affect the navigation of either the Hope or the Aquarius. These two ships, the only vessels involved in this collision, were aware of each other for many miles and knew of their respective obligations.

We modify the judgment of the district court insofar as it holds Aquarius 20% liable for this collision, and direct that judgment be entered exonerating Aquarius and holding Hope solely at fault.

TUG OCEAN PRINCE v. UNITED STATES
584 F.2d 1151 (1978)

Oil barge which was being towed in Hudson River channel collided with submerged rock causing oil spillage. Owner of tug sought exoneration or limitation of liability. Barge owner sought indemnity from tug owner for fines imposed on it under the Federal Water Pollution Control Act, and Government sought cost of pollution cleanup and imposition of civil penalty on barge owner. Actions were consolidated for trial and the United States District Court, for the Southern District of New York, Gerard L. Goettel, J., 436 F.Supp. 907, held that tug owner was entitled to limitation of liability, and all parties appealed. The Court of Appeals, Mehrtens, Senior District Judge, sitting by designation, held that: (1) tug owner's failure to appoint a captain and to post a lookout was not only negligent but was in violation of statutory duty and, thus, tug owner would not be entitled to limitation of liability as to cost of tug, and (2) tug owner's failure to inform one pilot of other pilot's unfamiliarity with river, its failure to appoint a captain, and its failure to require a lookout under the circumstances constituted willful misconduct so that owner's liability to the United States for pollution cleanup costs would not be limited.

Reversed in part, affirmed in part and remanded.

. . .

Before OAKES, Circuit Judge, BLUMEN-FELD, Senior District Judge, MEHRTENS, Senior District Judge.

MEHRTENS, Senior District Judge:

The oil-laden Barge New London, push-towed by the Tug Ocean Prince, struck a charted rock outside the navigable channel in the Hudson River, sustaining damage and causing a considerable oil spill. Tug Ocean Prince, Inc. and Red Star Towing & Transportation Co. (Red Star), the owner and charterer of the Tug Ocean Prince, petitioned for exoneration from or limitation of liability under 46 U.S.C. § 183 *et seq.* in which proceeding Pittston Marine Transport Corp. (Pittston) filed claims for damage to the barge and loss of cargo. Red Star thereafter filed a third-party action against the United States of America (the United States), alleging that its fault caused the casualty. The United States counterclaimed against the tug and crosclaimed against the barge for the pollution cleanup expenses. Pittston crossclaimed against the United States for its damages and the United States counterclaimed against Red Star for the money spent for cleanup. The United States also filed a separate action against them for the cleanup costs in the civil pollution penalty under 33 U.S.C. § 1321. The actions were consolidated for trial. The trial court denied exoneration but granted limitation to the value of the tug. It further found that Pittston was not responsible for the oil spill and dismissed the United States' action against Pittston. The court also dismissed both Red Star's and Pittston's claims in the third-party action as well as Pittston's counterclaim against the United States in the action it instituted to recover the cleanup costs, limiting the tug's liability for pollution cleanup to $100 per gross ton under the provisions of 33 U.S.C. § 1321. Nobody is happy and everybody has appealed.

The court below made detailed findings of fact and conclusions of law. *The Ocean Prince v. United States*, 436 F.Supp. 907 (S.D.N.Y.1977). The facts may be capsulated, enlarging upon them as need be in the discussion that follows.

THE FACTS IN THE COURT BELOW

In examining Pittston's and the United States' contentions that the district court erred in holding that Red Star was entitled to limit its liability, we make plain at the outset that we accept the fact-findings made by the trial court except where they are inconsistent or, in our opinion, clearly erroneous.

The Tug Ocean Prince has an overall length of 94.7 feet, a gross tonnage of 198 tons, and her deep draft was about 14 feet. She is pilothouse controlled, equipped with radar, a gyro-compass, a magnetic compass, and a searchlight. She did not have a pelorus or azimuth circle or other equipment with which to take visual bearings. The radar had relative graduations. With the cursor or cross hairs relative bearings could be taken. The tug's deck crew consisted of two pilots, Walter Reimer and John Kiernan, both Coast Guard licensed, and two deckhands, one assigned to each watch. Each pilot and deckhand stood six-hour watches. The deckhands had other duties and were often sent below for coffee, all of which was well known to Red Star's Vice President of Operations.

The tank Barge New London, of 1665 gross tons, has an overall length of 295 feet, and was drawing 12 feet. In her stern was a pushing notch where the bow of the tug fits snugly. The tug was secured to the barge with steel cables and synthetic lines. Steering and propulsion were supplied by the tug.

Operating as a unit, the tug and barge were 385 feet long, of 1863 gross tons.

Reimer had been employed by Red Star for about one and one half years while the Ocean Prince operated in southern waters. In southern waters Reimer had acted as her captain and mate, but when the Ocean Prince came north at the beginning of the year Reimer left for vacation.

Kiernan was employed by an associated company as tug captain. He had extensive experience on the Hudson River, but, except for this voyage, had never worked for Red Star. On February 1, 1974, Kiernan joined the Ocean Prince as mate.

On February 2nd the permanent captain of the Ocean Prince left and thereafter Reimer arrived. Red Star intended Kiernan to be captain and Reimer to be mate, but Red Star's dispatcher, who assigned the Ocean Prince to the job, did not communicate this information to Kiernan or to Reimer, and neither had anyone else, nor was the fact that Reimer had never piloted on the Hudson River communicated to Kiernan. As a result, Kiernan and Reimer each assumed that he was the mate and the other the captain. Reimer, although he had no experience on the Hudson River, did not check the navigation aids on board or examine the Light List or the Coast Pilot very carefully.

About one and three-quarters miles north of Bear Mountain Bridge lies a large submerged rock formation on the west side of the channel, which is clearly indicated on the chart and marked in winter months by the unlighted black can buoy "25".

The Light List warns the pilot not to rely on floating aids to navigation; that all buoys should be regarded merely as warnings or guides; that whenever, if possible, a vessel should be navigated by bearings or angles on fixed objects on shore and by soundings rather than reliance on buoys; that the lighted buoy "25" is replaced by an unlighted can buoy from December 15 to April 1; and that the fixed light "27" on Con Hook Island is on a black skeleton tower 46 feet above water.

The Coast Pilot advises pilots that during the ice season aids to navigation are covered or dragged off station by moving ice; that, however, the river is well marked by lights along the shore and, most important, that with respect to the rock marked by buoy "25", the rock has a depth of seven feet, and with a fair current there is a tendency to set toward the rock; caution is advised.

At about 1800 hours (6:00 P.M.) Red Star's dispatcher advised the Ocean Prince to proceed to Exxon Dock to take the Barge New London to

Kingston. Nothing was said about who would be the captain or Reimer's lack of experience on the Hudson River. The Ocean Prince proceeded there, was secured to the barge, after which Reimer went below and Kiernan continued on watch. At 2330 hours (11:30 P.M.) Reimer came to the pilothouse and relieved Kiernan of the watch. The tug and barge continued northward up the Hudson River past Peekskill and approached Bear Mountain Bridge. The tide was ebbing. There was ice in the river and visibility was about two miles with snow flurries. The tug was proceeding at a speed of about six knots over the bottom. The radar was operating and a chart for the area was in the wheelhouse. When the tug and barge passed under the bridge, Reimer sent the deckhand down to the galley to get coffee, remaining by himself in the wheelhouse.

Although able to see both shore lines of the river, Reimer began using the tug's seachlight to look for buoy "25" on the lefthand side of the channel. Unable to see it, he reduced the engine speed to "half, maybe less" and continued searching for the buoy. He never saw the light on Con Hook Island ahead, although it was visible from a position off Fort Montgomery or Town of Manitou about 1.5 miles south of the light and one mile south of the point of striking. The deckhand returned to the wheelhouse about the time that the barge struck the rock on her port side and to the left of the navigational channel. Oil escaped from the damaged cargo tanks, creating a serious pollution problem. Reimer never saw the can buoy. Kiernan came to the wheelhouse shortly after the striking, saw the Con Hook Island light ahead and observed the can buoy on the starboard beam of the tug 50 to 75 feet away. Reimer was very upset

and Kiernan took over the wheel. He turned the tug and barge around and headed south to the Dayline Pier. After turning around Kiernan observed the lights on the Bear Mountain Bridge about two miles away. . . .

THE FAILURE
TO POST A LOOKOUT

[15] The district court, while finding that "Reimer failed to post a lookout when the conditions were such that the same was required," also found that "There was no proof whatever that a lookout forward could have observed the ice stranded buoy," and then it concluded that "the failure to post a lookout cannot be said to have contributed to the collision." This we find to be clearly erroneous because a lookout of suitable experience and competence, properly stationed, and vigilantly employed in the performance of his duty would have seen and reported the Con Hook Light in ample time to avoid the casualty.

Title 33, U.S.C. § 221 reads as follows:

Nothing in these rules shall exonerate any vessel, or the owner or master or crew thereof, from the consequences of any neglect to carry lights or signals, or of any neglect to keep a proper lookout, or of the neglect of any precaution which may be required by the ordinary practice of seamen, or by the special circumstances of the case.

The importance of a lookout was stated by the Supreme Court in *The Ariadne*, 13 Wall. 475, 80 U.S. 475, 478–79, 20 L.Ed. 542 (1861), thus:

The duty of the lookout is of the highest importance. Upon nothing else does the safety of those concerned so much depend. * * * It is the duty of all courts charged with the administration of this branch of our jurisprudence, to give the fullest effect whenever the circumstances are such as to call for its application. Every doubt as to the performance of the duty, and the effect of non-performance, should be resolved against the vessel sought to be inculpated until she vindicates herself by testimony conclusive to the contrary.

[16, 17] The lookout rule applies, of course, to tugboats. . . . It is also established that the pilot steering a tug and tow is not a proper lookout. . . .

Reimer was alone in the wheelhouse some 1750 yards south of the location of the charted rock when he experienced difficulty in locating the buoy. Despite being unable to locate it visually or with the radar, he did not direct the deckhand to serve as a lookout. The uncontradicted evidence shows that Con Hook Light was visible about 0.62 miles or 1300 yards south of the rock marked by buoy "25". From that point it would have taken the tug and barge 10 to 12 minutes to reach the rock all while the Con Hook Light and the shore line were visible.

The Con Hook Light is on top of a tower 46 feet above mean low water. It is visible at the rock (buoy "25"), is visible off Mystery Point, at Manitou, and is visible further south. The chart shows that there is a straight line of sight from Con Hook Light all the way down to the center of the Bear Mountain Bridge.

This is where the failure to have a proper lookout is important and significant and not his ability or inability to see the buoy. Once Con Hook Light was sighted, a pilot could take bearings forward to that light and aft to Bear Mountain Bridge, establishing a line of position and a danger bearing so that the tug's position on one side would assure the tug and barge being in safe waters, while a position on the other side would clearly indicate a hazardous situation. Reimer had at least 10 minutes and probably more time during which the Con Hook Light was visible, yet he had no lookout and did not notice it himself. Even though a lookout did not see the ice stranded buoy, it would be a matter of pure speculation to say that a proper lookout would not have seen and reported Con Hook Light.

It seems clear that under the circumstances existing the ordinary practice of seamen required the keeping of a proper lookout at that time and place. Of course, in order to take proper precautions Reimer would first have to see Con Hook Light. He did not see it, and there was no lookout to report it, as the person who would have been the lookout was getting coffee. This was the usual practice condoned by Red Star's Vice President of Operations.

[18] The failure to post a lookout when the conditions were such that the same was required was not only negligent and contrary to good practice, it was also a violation of a statutory duty. Such a violation invokes *The Pennsylvania* rule. When a ship violates a statutory rule intended to prevent casualties "The burden rests upon the ship of showing not merely that her fault might not have been one of the causes, or that it probably was not, but that it could not have been. Such a rule is necessary to enforce obedience to the mandate of the statute.". . . The "Pennsylvania rule" is still alive and well today. That rule's vitality and force were not in any degree affected by *United States v. Reliable Transfer Co.*, 421 U.S. 397, 95 S.Ct. 1708, 44 L.Ed.2d 251 (1975), which overruled *The Penn-*

sylvania only in so far as it abolished the Mutual Fault-Equal Contribution rule and substituted a new rule requiring liability for collision damage to be allocated proportionately to the comparative degree of fault.

[19] In this case we hold that the district court's finding that failure to post a lookout cannot be said to contribute to the casualty is in the light of the uncontradicted facts and *The Pennsylvania* rule clearly erroneous and that Red Star failed to over-come its burden of showing that by all reasonable probabilities its failure to require a lookout did not contribute to the cause of the collision. We further conclude that a finding of lack of privity or knowledge on Red Star's part is also clearly erroneous.

This alone is enough to deny Red Star limitation of liability. . . .

Reversed in part, affirmed in part, and remanded for further proceedings consistent with this opinion.

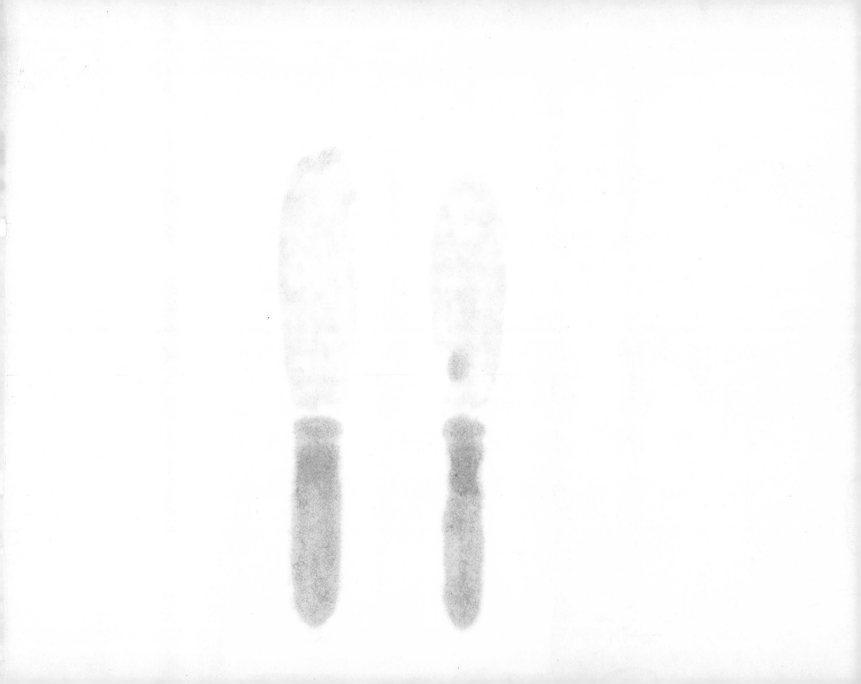

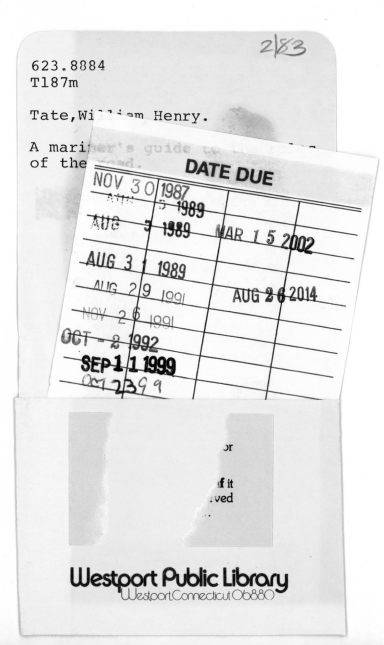